MW01525989

THE
RED PILL
BOOK

A PRACTICAL GUIDE TO LIVING YOUR BEST LIFE

JOSEPH HORROCKS

◆ FriesenPress

Suite 300 - 990 Fort St
Victoria, BC, V8V 3K2
Canada

www.friesenpress.com

ISBN
978-1-5255-1017-5 (Hardcover)
978-1-5255-1018-2 (Paperback)
978-1-5255-1019-9 (eBook)

1. SELF-HELP, PERSONAL GROWTH

Distributed to the trade by The Ingram Book Company

THE RED PILL BOOK:
A PRACTICAL GUIDE TO LIVING YOUR BEST LIFE

Unlock yourself from the ties that bind you. Learn how to harness the immense power of your subconscious mind through meditation and change your physical reality. If you wake up happily content with love in your heart and gratefulness for the life you've been gifted, then you're already as rich as it gets.

Don't just wish and dream. Take action! We are all dreamers. Every one of us. Everything that gets created by people in the physical world must first be imagined. But to bring dreams and thoughts to fruition of reality, you must make a plan for that to happen and then follow through on your plan. "Wishing will not bring abundance in life. But desiring abundance with a state of mind that becomes an obsession, then planning definite ways to acquire those things you want through goal setting and backing those plans with a persistence that does not recognize failure, will bring you what you desire".Napoleon Hill, Think and Grow Rich

TABLE OF CONTENTS

The Red Pill Book: a practical guide to living your best life 5

Foreword by the Author 9

Introduction 11

Chapter 1 Get to Know Yourself 17

Chapter 2 The Twelve Universal Laws 25

Chapter 3 Self-improvement Skills, Kill Your TV, and Start
Building Your Library 39

Chapter 4 Daily Exercises in the Law of Attraction 61

Chapter 5 It's Meditation Time, Yo! 77

Chapter 6 Healthy body ... Healthy mind. The Importance of
Mind and Body Alignment for Commanding the Law of Attraction 93

Chapter 7 Get Happy. Forgive Everybody. Be Grateful. Embrace
the Power of Love. Start Giving 103

Chapter 8 The Superchargers of the Law of Attraction 115

Chapter 9 The Conscious and Subconscious Mind: Applying the
Law of Attraction 131

Chapter 10 The Science of Mind Power 145

Chapter 11 Money May Not Buy Happiness but Having Lots of it
Certainly Doesn't Suck 165

FOREWORD BY THE AUTHOR

The wool has been pulled over your eyes to blind you from the truth. We are all born slaves into a prison that cannot be seen, tasted, smelled, or touched.

> Red pill or blue pill?
> "The Matrix 1999"

I warn you. This is your last chance to remain in wonderland. For, if you read through this book, the side of life that has been concealed and hidden from you will now be revealed with life-changing consequences.

Let's explore three major truths in life
   1. You're going to die
   2. You don't know the time or place.
   3. You can influence your destiny and manifest your reality with the immense power of your subconscious mind.

Welcome Reader! And thank you so much for purchasing the Red Pill book. How far down does the rabbit hole go, you might ask? Well in human terms, we don't actually know, but new discoveries in science tell us the possibilities are mind-boggling.

Let me introduce myself. My name is Joseph Horrocks. I was born and raised on the west coast of Canada in beautiful British Columbia. I grew up on Saltspring Island, which is a true island paradise; and for me, will always be home. I currently live in Vancouver, run a successful renovation company, and have a deep interest in metaphysics.

Within the pages to come is very powerful information. Everything you need to fulfill your highest aspirations, wishes, and dreams. Within these pages lies the key to a higher state of consciousness and enlightenment. Or simply enjoy what I hope you will find to be an interesting read. It's all up to you.

Like mastering a musical instrument, empowering your mind involves dedication and lots of practice. A child can sit at a grand piano and make some sounds plunking away at the keys. But a virtuoso concert pianist can pull up to the very same instrument and push it to its outermost limits and capacity. If you're willing to put in the time with dedication on a daily basis, the positive results of personal mind power are a foregone conclusion.

Repetition is very much the theme of my book. Many ideas will be repeated to plant seeds through the important phrases and theories that will be reinforced throughout the book in various ways.

Also, to achieve the full benefit of the book, it needs to be read again and again and again. Up to 100 or more times if you're up for it.

P.S. I love my swear words. I use them to punctuate certain phrases and sentences. At the risk of coming off not as polished as other writers – this is me, folks!

INTRODUCTION

Why did I decide to name my book *The Red Pill Book*? The book's title is a reference to the movie, *The Matrix*. The movie depicts a dystopian future, in which reality as perceived by most humans, is actually a simulated reality called "The Matrix". The Matrix world is created by sentient machines to subdue the human population, while their bodies' heat and electrical activity are used as an energy source.

TIME TO UNPLUG FROM THE MATRIX

I believe the movie's depiction of the human race is more fact than fiction. I believe that, just like in the movie, we are all plugged in and programmed to "The Matrix". However, I also believe that with the proper implementation of the practices and information presented in this book, they can surely release you from the ties that bind you. In modern day culture, these ties repress and suffocate your true potential for happiness and abundance to reach whatever it is that defines your hopes, dreams, and aspirations in life. In the movie, the blue pill keeps you hypnotized and plugged into the Matrix forever. The red pill unplugs you from The Matrix and releases you to live your true life. I would suggest to you that metaphorically I urge you: it's time to choose the Red Pill.

I would suggest that for most of you, you do not know that you do not know. The best place I believe to start in this process is in the knowledge that you do not know what "you do not know". I would emphasize to you that you are not living the real you. You do have the potential to live the real you though; to unplug and explore who you really are, and live the real you. But right now you are living the grand sum of others' beliefs and habits. Hypnotized, spinning around blindly in the Matrix, on mental autopilot.

And I would suggest within these pages lies the key to wake up to a higher consciousness of reality, to become self-aware, to realize true enlightenment, to unplug from the Matrix and reprogram yourself to a better, higher, functioning, more content you.

Look around you. Wherever you live, whatever circle of society you are part of, you will notice that the vast majority of people live and focus on the world outside of themselves; they roll with punches and are manipulated by "the world without". Those who are more enlightened, however, are intensely involved with "the world within".

In daily life, there are all kinds of things going on all around us, and there are things going on within us internally. The key message is that if you want to control the things going on in the world without you must master and channel from the world within. Most people focus on the world without, but if you strive to become self-aware and enlightened you will become intensely involved with the world within. Your thoughts, feelings, visualizations whether good or bad, positive or negative are the organizing principles of your life experience. It all starts from your world within and your immensely powerful mind and manifests to the physical reality of your world without.

IT'S A SCIENTIFIC FACT

The potential is yours to directly and intentionally control the world without by tapping into the infinite power within that is gifted to every human being on the planet. This is no longer just a theory but proven scientific fact. I am talking about your subconscious mind. It never takes a break. As we think so we are, the difference is you can choose to control and channel your subconscious mind to create the reality you desire.

This book is about personal discovery and the opportunity to lose the old you and embrace a new you. This book is about change and empowerment. Many people when introduced to the theories and practices of Mind Power/Law of Attraction, pooh-pooh it immediately, saying their lives are fine and don't need that hippie-dippy new age voodoo bullshit; that it's a scam to make the people flogging it, rich.

For those that have that mindset, which was many of my friends and acquaintances, everyone is of course entitled to their opinion. I would look at the example of how they were living their lives thinking, *Jesus! If they would just give it a try they could benefit so much*. But the best thing about this life is the free will to do whatever it is we want to do. My issue here is that I don't believe people realize just how much this matrix of spiritual repression actually exists.

I'm sure many of the people reading these words are thinking, *Yes the media, etc. are trying to manipulate how we think*. Obviously, but don't let themselves go so far as to accept that your subconscious mind has been completely programmed with self-sabotaging, repressive, self-defeating ways of thinking and living; to believe in a model of other people's beliefs and values and culture more for their benefit than yours.

I believe for most folks there exists a matrix of harmful paradigms and negative neural pathways riddled throughout your subconscious mind. They are well engrained throughout all your years of living and absorbing them, and they are stubborn. They need to be pulverized, broken down, and expelled from your subconscious mind so that you can rebuild through the process of neural plasticity powerful new neural pathways that serve your wishes and desires.

According to MedicineNet.com, "Neural plasticity is the brain's ability to reorganize itself by forming new neural connections throughout life. Neural plasticity allows the neurones (nerve cells) to adjust their activities in response to new situations or to changes in their environment."

Being equipped with a subconscious mind that is rewired to serving your hopes, dreams, and aspirations as opposed to other people's is the point that defines the equivalent of fully unplugging from the matrix.

These theories have been around for years and were first introduced by Napoleon Hill, in his book, *Think and Grow Rich*, and Earnest Nightingale's, *Strangest Secret*. With new discoveries in the field of Neural Science and Quantum mechanics/physics, there is actual proof that all of what I'm saying here is true and possible. These badass paradigms and negative neural pathways are comparable to good old Satan, the Devil, in that their single greatest feat is that most people don't believe or know they exist.

They are persistent and stubborn. If they catch wind that you have become aware that they do actually exist, and that it's time to give them the boot out of your subconscious mind space, they go into survival mode and start putting on the moves, dodging and diving and doing whatever they can to stay in control. You need to crush the self-limiting, self-sabotaging paradigms and harness the true God-given awesome power that lies within your subconscious mind. I will show you exactly how to do this.

There are two main actions you need to engage in. The first is eradicating the negative beliefs and neural pathways engrained in the present state of your subconscious mind. Break it down and rebuild a newly empowered, rewired, subconscious mind. This is done through daily meditation and mind power exercises, sending messages and direction to your subconscious mind by way of your conscious mind. The second step is learning the tools and practices for how you can move mountains with the immense power of your subconscious mind once you've mastered it, which I will also present throughout the course of this book.

To become truly proficient in projecting the power of your subconscious mind, you must first understand its principles (Chapter 9). Learn why and how your subconscious mind is the most powerful source in the universe truly believe that and then master and implement that power

The idea behind the Law of Attraction is that thoughts become things. You can get what you want by thinking about it. They call this, The Secret. The statement is true but there is a lot more to the process than what is explained in the movie, *The Secret*. The best-kept secret from the masses is not time travel, Black Holes or ColdFusion. It is the fact that the human mind is a very powerful transmitter and receiver. With practice, you can learn how to increase the transmissions of your subconscious mind with intense focus and a high rate of vibration to then tap into the quantum field and literally change and modify things in the physical world. This great power lies within every one of us, waiting for us to give it development and expression. You do not have to acquire this power. You already possess it within your subconscious mind. You simply need to learn how to activate and use it.

With practice and mastery of thought projecting with high vibration, you can achieve any task, goal, dream, reality that your mind can think of combined with a burning desire, persistence, faith, and belief that you can make it so. If this piques your interest, keep on reading, and I will show you the methods how.

The thought of this may make your heart race a bit, and think, *Holy crap, that's some mind-blowing crazy good stuff!* Then all your matrix programming kicks in and says it's bullshit. Get real! The biggest hurdle is that we live in a time where everyone wants to get stuff now and quick. People will try for a little bit and say where are the miracles? It doesn't work. It's bullshit.

IT'S UP TO YOU

For true life-changing results, daily practice is essential. Unfortunately, it isn't as easy as taking a little red pill to truly become unplugged from the Matrix. It will take considerably more effort, involving a lot of daily practice. The daily practice is key to bit by bit, with incremental steps, reverse years of negative unconscious conditioning. If we want to use a harsher word we could say brainwashing. You truly need to stay the course and put in the time and dedication. I will provide you with everything you need to make it happen but it's of course ultimately up to you. It's been said that only three or four out of every one hundred people in this life go as far as to have both a definite purpose and a definite plan for the attainment of that purpose. It was said almost 80 years ago by author Napoleon Hill and it's as true today as it was then. Thus proving the road to enlightenment, my friends, is truly the path not much traveled.

Very few people take the time to set goals, write them down and document them and fewer still speak them aloud daily in front of a mirror with passion, belief, and conviction! I recommend this practice. At first, it can seem a little weird, but if you can have the discipline to engage in this daily routine you will be far and above the rest of the pack.

Shine the sun's light through a magnifying glass if you move the glass around, not much happens. But steady it, focused on one spot, at the right trajectory, and it can start a fire. You can do the same with your mind if you train it right with daily practice and then intensely focus on what it is you really want that would make your life happy and fulfilling

At first, it doesn't matter if you know the exact science of why and how things work. Just trust me that it works and follow along and absorb the information in the order that it's presented in the book. I'm not going to boast or claim that my book will reveal some unprecedented super system or that it's the only way success can be properly achieved. All I'm saying is that I know these practices for sure work, and if you apply them on a daily basis, you can most certainly have life-changing success.

CHAPTER 1
GET TO KNOW YOURSELF

Who are you really? Ask yourself this question honestly. Until you know who you are for real you can't come to terms about where it is you belong. Much of what drives the behaviour of how we perceive ourselves is the result of preconditioned subconscious attitudes and beliefs. It's important to go deep within in order to figure out how we truly see ourselves on a subconscious level. Once you have had the courage to put yourself in the crosshairs and do a deep and honest eye-opening self-analysis of who you are – your tendencies, strengths, weaknesses, good and bad habits, what is your true character and personality type – you can then get clear on why you're here, what is truly important to you, and just exactly what you want to accomplish with this miracle life you have been gifted. Yes, it truly is a gift, that's why it's unfortunate for the peeps that like the phrase, "Life is a bitch and then you die" or in the same vibe actor William H. Macy's character Frank Gallagher in the series Shameless: "The world is going to fuck you! All you can do is take it up the ass and soldier on."

Old Frank may have a point here, which is to say yes there are going to be trials, obstacles, challenges, heartbreak, and yes, in some cases, you might get reamed without the lube.

IT'S ALL A MATTER OF PERSPECTIVE
But that my friends is what makes life worth living and rewarding so soldier on we must and the glass half empty or full perspective is up to us. As Henry Ford said, "Whether you think you can or you think you can't you're right." How about life is fricking awesome and then

our eternal soul will pass on through the cosmic plain onto a new and magical mind-blowing beginning so gloriously and immensely mind-blowing that we can't even comprehend it given the minuscule amount to which we utilize our immensely powerful human brain at this point in time of human evolution. I think that sounds much better than 'life is a bitch then you die'. See folks, it's all a matter of perspective.

The fact is, we all have issues. It's part of being human.

For many of us, when we start digging around with the questions such as, Who am I? What is it that makes me think the way I do? Why do I react and do the things I do? We dig up a lot of negative stuff. It's for that reason many people don't want to go there. The fact is, we all have issues. It's part of being human. You need to have the courage to go deep within and examine all your strengths and weaknesses and develop a strategy for where you can improve.

When asking yourself the question who am I and what is it in life that will truly make me happy, and define my definite purpose, think to yourself what would you be if you knew:

- all obstructions in your way would be removed
- all the cooperation you need will materialize, and
- you can't possibly fail!

If you were on a date or a job interview how in a minute or less would you describe yourself: strengths and weaknesses. Ask the question, what matters to you? What are your core values? Define exactly what values are most important to you. Once you've defined your core values, ask yourself, what is it that will make you truly happy? And, finally ask yourself, how would your life be different if money was no object? Where and how would you live? What would your home look like? Would it be a waterfront property with a boat and private wharf out front? Would you own a Learjet? A ranch with horses? Have some fun with it.

Are you a generous person? Or a selfish person? Are you a complete asshole that nobody likes? Are you too conservative? Or are you too scattered trying too many things at once and not focusing on any one thing long enough to make any progress? Do you procrastinate? Let's take a look at you!

In Poker-Pro Phil Hellmuth's *Masters of Poker* series he uses animals to explain the character traits of the different types of people you might see at the gambling tables. Here is his interpretation and although he's talking about character traits and how they relate to gambling at the poker table these same character traits are observed in the way many people live and approach their daily lives.

THE MOUSE

"The mouse is an ultra-conservative player who plays very strict starting hand requirements. The mouse will bet, but rarely ever raises a bet or re-raises. The mouse almost never bluffs. If a mouse actually does raise or re-raise, it probably means they have an almost unbeatable hand."

The problem with the mouse is that he is too cautious and scared to take any risks. He is too predictable and will win some small pots, have some successes but never get the big payouts.

THE JACKAL

"This type of player plays a lot of cards, and bets and raises with abandon. He is the direct opposite of the mouse. The jackal's chip stack often resembles a roller coaster ride, as it will climb when he has great cards, and then falls back to near nothing when he has a string of bad cards".

They play loose, and bluff with trash hands. They have the potential to win some big pots but will never keep them because of their reckless play.

THE ELEPHANT

"The elephant is what most poker players refer to as a 'calling station.' The elephant has loose starting hand requirements, and so he plays in a lot of pots. As a result, he ends up in a lot of hands that he or she has no chance of winning. The elephant is content to call his hand to the river, even when common sense tells him he's been beaten".

Trying out almost every opportunity that crosses their path, the Elephant can't get ahead because he is all over the place with too many dance partners and not enough focus on winning hands and strategy.

THE LION

After he gives the rundown of the mouse, jackal, and elephant, Phil explains that in poker, as would be in life, "the lion is the most success-ful because he combines the restraint and cautious play of the mouse with the risk-taking traits of the jackal, but calculated risks, as opposed to reckless ones like the jackal. He takes his time to pick the profitable opportunities following a carefully charted strategy for success."

In life, we need to be like the lion. You can't stay stuck at the start-ing gate, too scared of your own shadow, to take the risks and get out there. But you've got to be smart and calculated, not reckless in your risk-taking. The lion's world does not entertain the time wasting that the elephant involves themselves in, by chasing every opportunity with resources too stretched out to realize any one of them to a big payout. So, yes folks. We all want to strive to be like the lion. And because we're all so different, each person's strategy will vary.

SELF-ESTEEM

We are always growing and changing based on our personality and life experiences. Let's take a look at your level of self-esteem.

Self-esteem is a big one! The truth is that we are all vulnerable and fragile in some way. Millions of people are subject to thoughts of anxiety, self-loathing and thoughts of being not good enough. It's been said that on average it takes 15 compliments to counterbalance a single negative putdown.

Let's start by examining your childhood; the time to when our entire negative neural pathways and destructive paradigms were first established. These paradigms drive our behaviour, self-perception, atti-tudes, and beliefs.

How were you treated? Were you repressed by the classic "children are to be seen and not heard"? How were you treated by parents and people in your environment? Were you treated respectfully and listened to or disrespectfully and harshly criticized?

> The most important relationship in your life is the relationship that you have with yourself.

Do you feel your emotional needs were given proper attention and nurturing or do you feel you were neglected? Were your accomplishments recognized or kicked to the side like you never achieved anything worthy of acknowledgement? Do you have any memories of suffering any mental, verbal, or physical abuse?

The most important relationship in your life is the relationship that you have with yourself. Starting with the relationship you have with yourself is the foundation from which all your other relationships are built, and a driving force in your choices and behaviours.

What would you see if you were to jump out of your body and look back down at yourself?

What is your confidence level? How do you think others view you?

What does your inner voice say to you?

Your inner voice is either telling you good things about yourself or bad things about yourself. People with healthy self-esteem will hear the voice that reassures them, telling them they are good to go and whatever the challenge "you've got this". On the other side of the spectrum, people with low self-esteem will hear the more critical "give it up, you're not worthy or good enough" self-loathing inner voice.

Examine if you have low or healthy self-esteem.

A person with healthy self-esteem believes that he or she is worthy. They don't over think or analyze things beating themselves up for small shortcomings, which comes part and parcel with every human experience. They generally keep an upbeat and positive good feeling about themselves and are pleasant to be around. They exhibit high levels of competency and a skill set to succeed in life.

Alternatively, a person with low self-esteem often delves into the pits of negative outlook and self-analysis of "me no good, me not worthy" and constantly seeks out other people's approval. Like people with healthy self-esteem, they want to be successful but subconsciously sabotage themselves by holding lower expectations, judging things harshly, and avoiding risk.

If you feel you're a person of low self-esteem then you may well want to turn this around and systematically replace the "I'm not good enough" mentality with healing doses of self-acceptance. It takes more than speaking positive affirmations aloud to deal with more extreme cases of low self-esteem. You should get more in-depth and seek out one-on-one help with a professional who can identify what is unique about your condition of low self-esteem and how to strategize the process towards healthy self-esteem for yourself. Seek counseling with a Cognitive Behavioural Therapist (CBT) professional.

We had some fun looking at the poker player personality types. Let's get more in depth with the question what is your personality type? Let's start with what is known as the "Big 5" personality traits.

1. **Extraversion:**

Folks that are Extraverts are excited, assertive, highly expressive, somewhat in your face type of people. They are high energy individuals. They are enthusiastic and like to drive the action.

2. **Agreeableness:**

The first thing that might come to mind is the phrase "yes man or woman", which implies someone who agrees and says yes to everything in a kiss-ass fashion forfeiting their own identity to be a faithful lapdog /human doormat.

But agreeableness can actually be a wise and strong character asset. This character trait can be prosocial, affectionate, helpful, generous, kind, and trusting and most of all, able to compromise and not be too rigid in their agenda or beliefs. Agreeable folks choose to have an optimistic view of human nature.

3. **Conscientiousness:**

People with this trait favour planned over spontaneous behaviour. They are high-level thinkers, organized, and pay attention to details. They are goal-oriented and do not play prey to their impulses.

4. **Neuroticism:**

These can be very dynamic individuals but often can be observed as insecure or emotionally unstable. They can be emotionally reactive, high anxiety and not handle stress well with the Negative Nelly, Wendy Whiner interpretation of ordinary situations as potentially disastrous and minor difficulties as insurmountable tasks.

5. **Openness to experience:**

These folks can be thought of as a bit "Whacko" in that they can tend to hold unconventional beliefs. They tend to be adventurous, willing to take a risk, have many interests, and they are both insightful and imaginative.

The best way to see where you fit among the Big 5 personality traits is to go onto the Internet and take an online Big 5 personality test. I encourage you to do some research and find which personality tests you prefer and then participate in two or three online tests.

The key to getting back the important information you need for self-analysis is that you must answer all the questions honestly. There are many good personality tests to be found online I would suggest starting with: The Myers & Briggs test found at www.myersbriggs.org and go from there.

CHAPTER 2
THE TWELVE UNIVERSAL LAWS

UNIVERSAL LAW 1: THE LAW OF DIVINE ONENESS

There is a lot of focus and attention given to the law of attraction but many people don't understand it is actually a secondary law.

The Law of Divine Oneness is a primary law and the most important law of the twelve universal laws.

The Law of Divine Oneness brings understanding to the reality that we are all global brothers and sisters with a divine nature, living in a world where everything is connected; everything we do, say, think and believe has an influence and ripple effect on others and our surrounding environment. Everything seen and unseen is connected.

In hippie terms, "Dude, everything is connected to everything and everyone is connected to everyone."

Pure consciousness or universal mind energy, the infinite intelligence the superconscious mind, the universe of parallel existence, the gum stuck underneath a bar stool. Everything is one and originated from and comprised of the same universal source energy. Before moving on, hold that thought and let it sink in and fuck with your mind a bit. Because understanding the oneness of everything is essential knowledge as we move forward to understanding the other universal laws and how they overlap and complement each other.

UNIVERSAL LAW 2: THE LAW OF VIBRATION

The Law of Vibration is also a primary law and second only to the Law of Divine Oneness. If you want to manifest your hopes and desires and tap into the unlimited power of your subconscious mind, then knowledge and understanding of the Law of Vibration is essential. It is for this reason, before moving forward through the other chapters, we get a good insight and understanding of the law of vibration and the crucial role it plays in every aspect of our existence and being.

The Law of Vibration states that everything in the Universe moves vibrates, and travels in circular patterns. Everything in existence seen and unseen, physical and nonphysical when analyzed in its most basic form, is made up of pure energy, which resonates in a state of vibration. And everything in existence has its own unique vibratory frequency or pattern.

Everything is energy and everything is in a state of vibration

Nothing sits still; everything within the universe/quantum field is in a constant state of motion; there is no such thing as an inertia.

> Our human subconscious mind is one of the very highest forms of vibration potential, our minds are the most powerful transmitter/receivers on the planet ...

Rates of vibration are known as frequency. From the lowest and the highest form of vibration the higher the frequency the more potent it becomes. Our human subconscious mind is one of the very highest forms of vibration potential, our minds are the most powerful transmitter/receivers on the planet and the funny thing is most of us don't even know it. I'm not making this up this is not some dipshit theory, it is a scientific fact. You need to know this, believe this, and then learn how to use this great power to your advantage.

Although things may appear to be nice and solid like a concrete brick, in reality when you look closer and break things down to their smallest components: molecules, atoms, neutrons, electrons, and quanta, everything that appears solid is energy vibrating at its own unique frequency. Denser objects have a higher rate of vibration and objects with lower density have a lower rate of vibration.

> Like attracts like.

The power and ability to create and manifest what you desire in life lies in the ability to link up your thoughts, actions, and habits to the matching vibrational frequency of what you want and attract those things into your life experience. Like attracts like. There is a vibrational version of everything you want waiting for you to achieve vibrational harmony with it. By the same token if you choose to live your life as the victim happy to gripe and complain that nothing ever works out, then you will in effect put yourself in vibrational harmony with all the shitty things you bitch about and attract exactly those things and circumstances into your life. Again like attracts like, easy peasy to understand but you'd be amazed how many people don't get it. If you're negative and talk shit about your life that's what you're going to get more of. Like two smokers that like to light up together, they both know it's a shitty negative addiction thing to do but having some company doing it helps them feel better about it. Often, you find people prop each other up in conversation about how shitty life is, the government is, the economy is, the weather is, you just can't win. Life is a bitch and we are all just waiting around to die, which will probably also suck a big bag of dicks. This camaraderie of negative commentary and conversation might put a smile on their face in the moment but ultimately just adds more powerful manifestation to what is their personal life shit show.

Ok, so let's say you get that and you're exclusively interested in riding the happy train of the universal vibrational harmony of the things you want. The big pitfall that traps many people is that they don't properly think through what they are wishing for and those things that they attract not only don't bring the happiness they sought but end up being a curse of disharmony and upheaval in their lives. It's so very important to know yourself before you start wishing and visualizing and then when you do start rubbing Aladdin's lamp with your requests, make damn sure it's carefully scrutinized and well thought out so it doesn't all blow up in your face down the road.

In the next chapter, I will introduce practices towards self-growth and improvement, which if followed will inevitably promote change in your life. When implementing change and imprinting beneficial new habits to your unconscious mind, it's good to understand what is at the root of your ability to change. And that is to raise your personal vibration and become self-aware.

It essential to start learning the process of mindfulness and will-fully raising your personal state of vibration and self-awareness, to get you in the right place mentally to begin the quest of self-growth and improvement.

What am I saying here? I'm saying self-improvement/growth should include the practice of daily meditation.

Good thoughts of prosperity and abundance or bad thoughts of worry and lack, our subconscious does not choose and does not distinguish between what is real and what is imagined; it says yes to everything. As the thoughts are presented it gets to work immediately sending and transmitting vibration.

Thought waves are cosmic waves they penetrate all time and all space.

Those times when you think of your friend and they call you right away is not a coincidence. When you think, oh I might spill this coffee on myself or I'm probably going to spill this coffee on myself and you spill that coffee on yourself it is not a coincidence.

You can put this power to the test the next time you need a parking space in a crowded suburban area. Quiet your mind and think to your-self repeatedly with confidence and belief, *my needed parking space will present itself to me in a timely fashion* over and over and sure enough your parking space will manifest. If it doesn't, that's not because it doesn't work it means your rate of vibration and projection was clouded and not 100% pure faith and belief in your mind power. Or to contradict the entire pretence and theme of my book for the sake of humour, maybe your parking space didn't manifest because on that day you were just plain shit out of luck to get a parking space. But give it a try and if you concentrate right, most of the time it should work. And yes folks, joking aside, if you concentrate exactly right it will always work. I bat an average of two parking spots from every three attempts, which is actually pretty good as I live in Vancouver where there is an insured car to equal every man, woman, and child in the city and a lack of parking spaces enough to drive anyone batshit crazy.

The power of your vibration transmissions is your link between mind and matter, between the physical state and the nonphysical state. By raising our state of consciousness through meditation and mind power practices we raise our awareness. The goal is to become highly self-aware, to master your conscious knowledge of your character, feelings, motives, desires and most of all to increase your mind power vibration to its highest possible rate, and to then have your subconscious mind blast it out to link up and align with the superconscious mind and transmute your goals and aspirations into physical reality within the quantum field.

This is the key to the whole spiel of the deal folks. The direction of your focus, emotions, habits, personality, and behaviour directly determines where you are going in life.

As you become more self-aware, stepping back and taking a close look at yourself, you will identify aspects of your personality and behaviour of which you were previously unaware. Having awareness creates the opportunity to make changes in behaviour and beliefs.

You can go within yourself and seek out and identify the negative, self-sabotaging neural pathways riddled throughout your subconscious mind so you can crush them and begin to physically rewire your brain through meditation and mind power exercises, to build and establish new powerful and positive neural pathways.

When we look creatively within ourselves in our inner world this is explained as a self-conscious state. We are aware of our objective as well as our subjective world.

There are many varying degrees of consciousness.

Divine consciousness would be the pinnacle – to reach divine consciousness and self-enlightenment – to become one with the creator/infinite intelligence.

Depending on where you sit on the scale of vibration and consciousness awareness is exactly what dictates where you are in life.

Many are not aware that they are not aware.

A person can have a doctor's degree or be a scientist; they could have a highly developed intellect but still have the low vibration of self-consciousness. People don't necessarily want to be this way but they simply don't know how to change it. Many are not aware that they are not aware.

Some people have a very high level of consciousness and awareness. These people have an exceptionally high rate of vibration. These people are not typically upset nor do they seem overly excited or depressed. They have learned the art of maintaining balance.

If a person is alone and lonely it's not because they want to be. If a person lives their lives uptight, repressive, regarded by their coworkers and people close to them as rigid and controlling ,an overall complete buzz kill of good vibes and not much fun to be around. It's not because they want to be it's because they don't know how to change it. C'est la vie ;)

The more you meditate and journey within yourself, and the more you study these principles, the higher your level of awareness.

You want to get unplugged from the Matrix, and you want to get tuned in to vibrational harmony between what it is you want and desire to manifest it within the quantum field. This is a worthy goal.

Everybody gets exactly what he or she's offering vibration ally. When we say everything happens for a reason, it sounds disconnected like an outside reason that has been assigned. Everything is happening because of the vibration offering that you are setting forth. Everything that is coming to anyone is coming in response to what they were thinking about. As you think a thought, it activates a vibration. As you continue to think, that vibration becomes stronger until eventually, it becomes a belief. A belief is just a thought you keep thinking. Once you have activated the vibration enough those vibrational patterns then match up and attracts those things that are at the same level of vibration. Like attracts like.

In life, we are not necessarily creating what we want but were creating exactly what we're thinking about

Generate the emotional good feeling response for vibration aligned with aspirations of what you want and practice it until you own it. If you keep offering the vibration of what you're currently living that's the momentum you've got going and that's what the universe is going to continue to bring to you. It's not a punishment but a direct reference of the vibration that you have established. You could establish a different vibration. The best chance you have at establishing a new vibration is when you first wake up in the morning you can choose to create your new reality or complain about your reality that's being created by default.

You are the instrument through which source energy flows to manifest what you want; understanding this is very important. You and the source energy are one, flowing through you in synchronistic vibrational harmony to manifest your desires. Understand that what you want is coming towards you asking you, do you really want me?

And if the answer is a passionate heart-centred yes then the infinite intelligence wants your success as much or more than you do.

With the concept of expectation comes expecting abundance. What we want to do is raise our level of awareness vibration frequency, so that the expectation becomes a natural state for our mind. To be in our mind, to be in expectation, is a mindset. It's a mental state that comes to you with an increase of awareness. The law of vibration explains the difference between mind and matter, between the physical state and the non-physical state of everything in the universe, which includes you and the nonphysical part of your personality where the mental magic takes place.

You already have everything you require to attract everything that you want into your life. If nothing is created or destroyed everything is already here in one state or another.

> Living in a state of grace with feelings of gratitude for all we
> have to be grateful for is an empowering daily practice.

Raise your awareness, become present in the now, realize source energy flows through you as its instrument of manifestation. It is a wonderful partnership and your most powerful ally. Your job is to define exactly what it is you desire, amp up your vibration to its highest frequency to make yourself a human magnet of attraction, tap into the source energy and then set it loose to manifest what you want, presenting the right inspirational ideas, people, circumstances and opportunities at just the right times they are needed. Lastly, once you understand the law of vibration, its principles, and how it works to move forward with a burning, passionate but confident expectation and desire, centre your ideas in your heart with belief as much as you do your mind. And last but not least, implement what I call the gratitude trick. Living in a state of grace with feelings of gratitude for all we have to be grateful for is an empowering daily practice. What is different about the gratitude trick is to embrace a feeling of gratitude for what you want with the mindset and feeling like you already have it before you actually have it. This will trick your subconscious mind to supercharge its manifest powers into action.

UNIVERSAL LAW 3: THE LAW OF ACTION

The Law of Action states that you must take action to perform the deeds necessary to achieve whatever it is you've set your sights on. Sounds straightforward and simple enough but the truth is many of us, including myself once upon a time, are procrastinating lazy ass mofos!

Visualization and dreaming of the good stuff you want is a great starting place but if you can't back your aspirations and follow through with actions then you will surely remain a dreamer at the starting gate. The difference between who you are and who you want to be is what you do, you need to set your goals, chart your action plan then follow through with a burning desire, persistence, faith, and belief that you will prevail.

Fear and procrastination are the evil twins at the ready to block your path to success. You need inspiration and a strengthened belief in your quest and that comes with becoming self-aware and raising and matching your personal frequency of vibration with those things that your aspire for. This action will magically bring forth into your life experience the events, people, and circumstances to help you towards your goals and add to your confidence and inspire you to work even smarter and harder.

When you take even the smallest action like writing out some basic goals and keeping a daily journal of activities towards their attainment, these small positive actions will have a resonating effect towards your life experience, and if you follow up day after day and imprint the actions to your mind so they become your habitual way of living. The good things that you want you will surely attract into your life.

UNIVERSAL LAW 4:
THE LAW OF CORRESPONDENCE

The law of correspondence speaks to the corresponding balance of how whatever is happening and all that you experience on the outside world is in direct correlation to what is happening and what you are experiencing within your inside world. Whatever is your outer world mirrors that of your inner world

As there is Ying there must be Yang. As is above so is reflected below.

Your good luck or bad luck, likeability, relationships, health, prosperity, your present station and environment in life are a direct reflection of your inner world.

If your inner thinking is immersed in and guided by the negative energy you can find yourself in a trap that will perpetuate a negative and unfulfilling life experience.

There is a direct link between your core values, your habits, how you think and feel on the inside, which in turn steers the ship to your life experience of how you feel and act on the outside. If you find yourself feeling crappy and bad on the inside then these inner feelings influence your perception of the outside world. If you can get yourself in a good place, a happy place with feelings of fulfillment through the practice of meditation, visualization, or simply engaging in activities that make you happy, then the good feeling you generate from the inside will manifest to you on the outside world. The results are guaranteed because of the law of correspondence.

UNIVERSAL LAW 5:
THE LAW OF CAUSE AND EFFECT

The Law of Cause and Effect states that every cause has an effect and every effect becomes the cause of something else. Throw a rock into the lake and resonating ripples are the result.

> "What we do in life echoes in eternity."
> —Maximus, *Gladiator* (2000).

> "There are no accidents."
> —Master Oogway, *Kung Fu Panda*

The universe is always in motion.

There is no such thing as rogue happenings by chance outside the Universal Laws. "What we reap is what we sow."

Every time we involve ourselves in thoughts, speech, or actions, we set off a frequency of vibration, a forward moving wave of energy throughout the universe, which then creates resulting effects and consequences either good or bad.

This is why a positive mindset, attitude, works, and deeds are important. As we do so we are, as we are – so we do. We create circumstances that align with the choices and actions we take. Be self-aware and create true balance in your life, don't dig yourself into a ditch of negativity, there is a lesson as simple as striving to be honest and real when everyone around you is seemingly getting away with lying their way through every situation.

I am reminded of Granny speaking of the "lie pie" saying basically you tell one lie then you got to tell another lie to cover for the previous lie and so on until you find yourself caught up and immersed in a big fat troublesome lie pie. You steer the ship and chart your path. Give good thought as to how you skip down the happy trail of life. Don't be false to others or yourself. So many people are two-faced, pretending, following the crowd, playing a part or just plain full of shit. Rather than the mercy white lie, it's better to sometimes leave certain information out of a conversation to avoid potentially hurting someone's feelings. But no matter what, strive to keep it real and be authentic for better or worse.

UNIVERSAL LAW 6: THE LAW OF COMPENSATION

You've heard the saying karma is a bitch, the Golden Rule "What goes around comes around" or "We reap what we sow."

This prophecy of compensation can swing both ways on the spectrum. If you've been a dick and built yourself up a nice bundle of bad shitty Karma by screwing people over and immersing yourself in negative energy, chances are the universe is going to fuck with you. But of course the reality is that you, as an instrument of the universe, are in fact fucking yourself, the universe is simply carrying out the deeds and follow through of the path and course you've set in motion.

By the same token, if you can live your life as an instrument of love, peace, joy, positive inspiration, and abundant generosity, you align yourself and find your life source frequency in vibrational harmony to receive blessings, miracles, and great prosperity. There is absolutely nothing wrong with being the receiver of great prosperity. The key to being a successful receiver, however, is in the talent and habit of being a master giver. Giving with the mindset of being happy to give selflessly, expecting nothing in return.

UNIVERSAL LAW 7: THE LAW OF ATTRACTION

At No. 7 we have the flashy Hollywood star of the universal laws garnering much global interest, attention, and discussion. Most successfully introduced to the masses through the movie *The Secret* this secondary universal law states in essence like attracts like. We can create and attract into our life experience people, circumstances, events, and things either good or bad through our thoughts, words, feelings, and actions. Do good get good, do bad get bad/the universal equivalent of your life experience mirroring getting reamed without the lube as our old friend Frank Gallagher would so graphically reminisce.

UNIVERSAL LAW 8: THE LAW OF PERPETUAL TRANSMUTATION OF ENERGY

Transmutation means "the action of changing or the state of being changed into another form. The energy of the Universe is always in a constant state of motion, warping and changing into and out of form. Always on the go in a state of motion, we can't ever stop it but we can control and direct it rather than letting it run amok through our life experience and our psychology. Ultimately, through meditation, we can slow things down and go deep within our being and rewire / transform our subconscious mind, crushing negative neural pathways and destructive self-sabotaging paradigms, replacing and transforming our subconscious with new positive neural pathways. Many people don't embrace change and like things to stay the same but this is naïve, for change is happening in every moment. You want to get ahead of it and ride and manipulate the wave to your benefit and avoid getting stuck on the gerbil wheel spinning blindly perpetuating all the same bad habits anchored in fear and procrastination.

UNIVERSAL LAW 9: THE LAW OF RELATIVITY

Throughout life, the universe will test you to see how badly we want what we want and to learn important lessons from such challenges. Roadblocks and setbacks can be a reason to quit or they can present inspiration to press forward.

Everything is relative in life. Our perspective for the quality or value of something is measured in relation to how we compare it to another object or situation. For example, how you view your quality of life. There is always someone out there that has it worse no matter how bad your situation, and no matter how successful you are there is always going to be someone more successful.

To put that thought into perspective here is a quote from *A New Earth* by Eckhart Tolle: "In form, you are and will always be inferior to some, superior to others. In essence, you are neither inferior nor superior to anyone. True self-esteem and true humility arise out of that realization. In the eyes of the ego, self-esteem and humility are contradictory. In truth, they are one and the same."

UNIVERSAL LAW 10: THE LAW OF POLARITY

The Law of Polarity states "everything can be separated into two wholly opposite parts, and that each of those still contains the potentiality of the other." The same as a car battery has two polar opposite posts there also exists two polar opposites of manifestation and intention. Everything is on a continuum and has an opposite – there is hot and cold, up and down, happy and sad, fast and slow, good and bad.

When immersed in darkness we can appreciate light, when faced with evil we can appreciate good and kindness, when lonely we can appreciate companionship.

The scientific term for the Law of Polarity is called wave-particle duality. Leading scientists in the study of quantum physics have discovered that light can behave in unpredictable ways. In one experiment, scientists can observe light display particle-like behaviour yet in another experiment it will display wave-like attributes, which brings us to the question: what is light? Is it a particle or is it wave? And the answer is that light is both.

If you're in a funk of bad thoughts and negative energy you can change your path and experience by focusing on the opposite: good thoughts and positive energy. To master and benefit from the law of polarity you must learn how to maintain physical and spiritual balance in your life. Proper diet and exercise, combined with stimulating and balancing your mind through meditation and relaxation, will help you remove yourself even if only for a few moments each day from the daily toil and distractions of the physical world.

UNIVERSAL LAW 11: THE LAW OF RHYTHM

The Law of Rhythm states that the energy in the universe is like that of a pendulum swinging back and forth. When universal energy swings to the right a certain distance it then must swing to the left the same distance. Everything in the universe is in a state of motion constantly vibrating swaying and flowing, swinging back and forth.

Like the tide coming in and out and the seasons coming and going everything in existence has a cycle, patterns, stages that move to a rhythm. All energy vibrates and moves according to a certain rhythm.

The Law of Rhythm is connected at the hip to the Law of Vibration. The Law of Vibration is the 600 horsepower V 8 engine with the Law of Rhythm being the Cadillac body that harnesses the power and takes it smoothly down the highway. As with every journey there are highs and lows. The key is to go with the flow and not let your emotions swing too far one way or the other. Don't be overly excitable or too easily disappointed/depressed.

Universal Law 12: The Law of Gender

The Law of Gender manifests in the animal kingdom as sex. Everything in nature is both male and female. For life to exist both are required. Feminine and masculine principles are at work in every facet of life manifesting on all planes of existence.

Also known as the Law of Gestation, it states that when we plant a seed (masculine/yang), it requires time and nurturing to grow and manifest (feminine/ying). You must learn patience and trust that the universe knows just what you need and when you will need it and present the people circumstances and events in a timely fashion custom fit for you. After planting the seeds of your ambitions, you must be patient and pair it up with persistence and an understanding that there needs to be a gestation period for you to get what it is you desire and wish for. Far too many give up and don't stay the course; often they give up right when the attainment of their goal is right around the next corner metaphorically speaking.

CHAPTER 3
SELF-IMPROVEMENT SKILLS, KILL YOUR TV, AND START BUILDING YOUR LIBRARY

Learn from your past, prepare and plan for the future, be and live in the present here and now. Raise your awareness and transmit to the infinite intelligence with your highest most concentrated frequency possible. Learn to set goals, improve your self-confidence/discipline, strive for personal excellence not perfection, be humble, don't make excuses and own your shit, go with the flow don't sweat the small stuff, know and understand that it's all small stuff, don't be an uptight rigid son of a bitch … oh yeah and kill your TV. Start building your library. That's the short version now here's the longer one.

They say wisdom comes with age but that's not necessarily the case, sometimes age comes alone. If you want to achieve wisdom with age you must be intentional about it. For self-growth and change, you must learn to be disciplined and motivated.

Here is the key to self-growth/improvement. Upgrade your life with continuous incremental change. Continuously identify small things that you can change leading to a dramatic improvement over time.

The key to successfully mastering manifestation of your dreams and aspirations is you have to be smart and put some dedicated thought into it. You can't just fall into it like a naive trusting puppy dog and convince yourself to quit your job and move to New York to be a Broadway performer if you can't sing or dance to save your life.

I am a huge believer in dreaming big where the sky is the limit, absolutely go for it and don't listen to the naysayers that prophecy your doom and failure but do listen to your intuition and work to your strengths to give yourself a proper fighting chance. If in fact your dream and passion is to be a Broadway performer and you have little to no talent but you've decided hell or high water this is your mission, then be smart and realistic about it. Don't quit your job and move to New York with $500 to your name. Take lessons part-time to see if you can develop some skill moving toward your goal.

If bit by bit you increase your confidence and skill and start kicking it then it may be time to make a bold move. And if you're not cut out for it that reality is going be clear to you through the process. The infinite intelligence combined with your intuition will guide you in another direction towards discovering a new area of personal strength that you can get behind and be passionate about.

When aspiring to attain the "Big Dream" the key is to first believe in your heart and soul that you can make it. So have a passion for it to get emotionally connected to the idea. Once you have developed a passion and a burning desire for the big goal you need to break it down into a succession of smaller short-term achievable goals.

Mapping out and achieving the smaller goals as you move toward the bigger goal will build your confidence and increase your belief that the process is real and actually works when put in action. Put another way, if you try to mow down your big power dream, and aspirations in one big chomp, you're going to stall out and choke on it. So break it down into chewable bites and you're good to go!

Many motivational speakers or self-improvement articles will urge you to set one big goal to become obsessive about it and work tirelessly until you achieve the goal, which is great advice. However, many and most people that have tried that approach have maybe achieved some partial success with the big goal approach but usually end in failure. There are many reasons for this failure; one main reason is that to make dramatic life-altering changes can be too overwhelming or just plain hurt.

It is better to change gradually and learn as you go.

If I tell a typical person today to stop eating meat and dairy products and adopt a vegan diet starting right now that person will feel sudden and serious pain even if he or she is entirely willing to follow my advice. The pain of this drastic change is likely to overcome the person's will to change, resulting in failure. For many people, just the thought of making such a major lifestyle change might prevent them from taking action. Large changes often include false assumptions where the action plan has not been carefully thought out and are therefore inherently destined for failure. For example, imagine if you quit your job to start earning money as a freelance photographer so that you will have greater freedom. At first, the action might be inspiring but you now find yourself going from 100% employed status to 100% self-employed status overnight, and you may not have anticipated the complexities of self-employment and quickly find yourself financially tits up. It is better to change gradually and learn as you go. Self-employment is a worthy goal but better to test your new endeavour in your spare time; do some trial and error before you quit your job and commit to it full time.

Step back and try to look at your life as an observer. Look at work/personal relationships, physical health, mental health, etc. and identify areas that need improvement. Observe yourself throughout a typical day, making a record of the problems or difficulties that you encounter. Even after completing a task successfully ask yourself how can I do that slightly better in the future.

> Understand that you are immaculately made, and you're not broken nor do you need fixing, you simply need to become centred and do some fine tuning.

Target areas to improve that you feel need priority attention and look for opportunities to make small improvements. If you have areas in your life that present big time obstacles and difficulty, know that you don't have to tackle and solve the whole problem at once. Each day, take incremental steps to make things slightly better. We tend to be impatient and want to fix entire problems immediately.

The better approach is to continuously make small improvements throughout your life, slowly but surely solving the adversity and challenges that come our way. You will be amazed by the compound effects of the many small improvements. Those who take the opposite approach – meeting large problems with drastic solutions often set themselves up for failure.

As long as you stay on track there are no failures there are simply attempts that don't work out and help assist you to find ways that will. Too many people think in terms of *I don't like the way I do this one thing, and I don't like my thinking or reactions to this or that situation and it needs fixing.* If you ever find yourself making the statement, *What the fuck is wrong with me?* This cultivates a deficiency consciousness and is entirely the wrong way of thinking. Understand that you are immaculately made, and you're not broken nor do you need fixing, you simply need to become centred and do some fine tuning.

Self-improvement is about making changes in your perceptions, beliefs, and habits. For many, it can mean a complete overhaul of your thinking and how you view and go about living your life. Change takes work, and there are plenty of forces and factors within your psychology working against you that want no part of the change and are perfectly content with the status quo.

The process of change requires learning and relearning. It requires breaking the habits of the old self and re-inventing a new self. In neuroscientific terms this is synaptic pruning to initiate lasting change. The pre-programmed bad habits and belief systems that you run on autopilot must be identified and eradicated. The first step is to be aware that the paradigms are real and controlling you until you forcibly shift your vibration and consciousness.

The paradigms are programmed within your subconscious mind and control what you do. If the paradigm doesn't shift the results don't change. If you continue to do as you've always done you'll continue to get as you've always got.

The paradigms are the programs that controls your habitual behaviour.

There is genetic programming and there is environmental pro-gramming. Physical daily practices are required like healthy living and exercise, goal setting and meditation.

Get well within yourself to identify the habits and ways of thinking that need to change at the very outset of your quest; this is done by focusing not so much on the past nor the future. There will be a time for focus and learning from past mistakes and accomplishments you've done well.

And there will be a time to focus on visualizing future events and the outcomes you desire. But at the outset, it is about raising your vibration and self-awareness and that is done through shutting out thoughts of past and future, quieting your mind and becoming focused on the present and tapping into very powerful and empowering uni-versal source energy to propel you on your way.

To get yourself primed and ready to employ mind power you're going to want to align your daily habits with the goal of self-growth and improvement.

This is how the word Schema (psychology) is explained in *Wikipedia:*

A schema (plural schemata or schemas) describes a pattern of thought or behaviour that organizes categories of information and the relationships among them. It can also be described as a mental struc-ture of preconceived ideas, a framework representing some aspect of the world, or a system of organizing and perceiving new information. Schemata influence attention and the absorption of new knowledge: people are more likely to notice things that fit into their schema while re-interpreting contradictions to the schema as exceptions or distort-ing them to fit.

Self-improvement is the same as reprogramming the schema scripts engrained within your subconscious mind and then channeling them to manipulate physical reality. This is the process of self-change and for many reasons people are fearful, reluctant, and lazy towards change. One major reason why change doesn't come easily is that you might get an exciting risky new thing in your mind that you want to try that might require a new positive routine and way of thinking. Such adventurous thoughts have to get by the gatekeepers of your conscious mind those being the negative, self-sabotaging paradigms deeply engrained within your subconscious thinking. They want nothing to do with exiting new risky things. They want to stay the course of safe uninspired good old status quo.

Just as in the movie *Star Wars* when Obi-Wan Kenobi said when being interrogated by the Storm Troopers, "These are not the droids you're looking for" the Paradigms will jump up wave their hand and say, "These are not the new and exciting things we've been looking for." Or, "This exciting risky new thing is not in our best interest." Or, "Perhaps tomorrow would be a good time to take another look at it for now let's get some yummy ice cream and watch TV."

Folks, these bad ass paradigms are tricky and stubborn and they hate change. The best way to get your mind to accept new habits and change is to pick a few areas of interest and start slowly.

When we get inspired it is important to act quickly and take action. By doing this we prove our conviction and belief in our desire. Taking action proves to the universe that you believe that you can have what you desire and that you're worthy.

We must take action to get what we want in our life, understanding when we take action we open up opportunities and pathways for things to flow into our life experience. If you sit on the couch and rub a genie lamp without taking action it's not likely you're going to bring the cool stuff that you want, into your life experience.

Get to the core of how you think the way you do. Most of what we believe to be true was brought into our lives and learned from our parents and culture mostly in our early childhood years when our brain is in the alpha /theta sponge, absorb mode. It shaped how we see the world then perpetuated and reaffirmed throughout adult life.

> To shift the paradigms, understand you must get to the core of why you think the way that you do.

Ask the question, *What I would have to believe is true to feel this way?* This way being the desired state of consciousness in achieving your goals.

Don't choose to be under the unconscious patterning of what we are thinking in the process. Become aware of what you believe to be true, become aware of what you're feeling and what instincts come to the surface, become aware of how each experience shapes your perspective.

It's very important to not get too serious or be too rigid in our desire. We must be in the moment and have a loose attitude about the vibration of our emotional set point. Things around us then become more malleable and formable. Take action, yes, but in a fun spirit let go and focus on feeling good and trust the infinite intelligence to get you there. Follow its lead to find the best pathway of least resistance.

Again, don't try to force anything, stop paddling upstream just embrace trust and feeling good and let the stream of the infinite intelligence universal source energy guide you. The obstacles in your path are on wheels and can be moved easily out of the way. There is a tendency for us to make them so much more than they need to be. The infinite intelligence knows exactly what is needed for your situation. Fall into it with trust and faith and love, feeling from your heart centre and watch the universal source energy knock itself out to bring you what you want.

Listen for clues and let yourself be guided.

Definite plans are important and so is taking action but listen for clues and let yourself be guided. As far as the path to get there, once you have projected to the universe where you want to go, let it run with it and try to stay out of the way.

The more general you are in your statement the less resistant it is. The more specific you are in your statement the more potential for resistance. This is not to say don't be thorough in mapping out your plan; this is to say be open to as to how the journey to success may carry you. And remember if you can't align the ideal with a heartfelt belief that it will manifest it never will.

There is a flow to your life. If you feel like you're struggling because you're trying to paddle upstream all you need to do is let go of your upstream strategy, stop going against the flow, trust in source energy, turn around the boat, stop paddling, and let the current take you where you naturally need to go.

I notice a lot of motivational speakers criticize the practice of "letting go" portraying it to be some wimp ass spiritual hippie strategy where you can stop taking action and trust the universe to supply all you need. Obviously, in my opinion, these people just don't get it, and they are the same motivational speakers that say there is no magical power out there waiting to link up with your subconscious mind to manifest your desires.

We are all entitled to our individual beliefs. For the record of how I feel about their perspective, they are categorically wrong and can feel free to pull the carrot out of their ass.

To be clear when I speak of "letting go" I'm speaking of letting go of bad habits, thoughts, beliefs, and paradigms that are screwing with your pursuit of happiness and abundance. I'm not saying to be so naïve as to throw your hands up and announce that you're ready for the universe to ship you happiness and abundance via transcendental express mail. I'm saying the infinite intelligence helps those who activate to help themselves. Understand developing a dedicated and disciplined work ethic is beneficial for sure but also keep in mind that working hard will not necessarily rule the day whereas working smart definitely will. Working smart does not just entail carefully thought out plans; it includes letting the universal source energy flow through you and use you as its instrument of manifestation for what you desire to achieve. Don't let go of taking action, don't let go of persistence and a passion to attain your ideals. Don't let go of your faith and belief that universal source energy is absolutely within you and at your side to yes "magically" help bring your aspirations to manifestation.

The beauty of mindful meditation is that while meditating you become present with the moment and your breathing and you let go of everything else. You quiet your mind and let go of all thoughts entirely, you let go of everything spinning around in your mind and consequently throughout your body, which for many is stress related, and focus solely on your breathing and become present at the moment.

Breathe in good spiritual energy and with every exhale release all the accumulated negative crap. This kind of letting go is the chicken soup for your soul and I believe everyone should practice peaceful, calming, healing energy of "letting go" in this way.

SKILL 1: KILL YOUR TV AND START ASSEMBLING YOUR LIBRARY

Step 1. Kill your TV! The master distractor must go! So many people arrive home, and the idiot box gets clicked on before they even take their shoes off. If you seriously want to get some things done in your life, at least for a while you need to feel the liberating experience of being television free. Don't toss it out the window where innocent bystanders may get crushed but the grandiose annihilation of your TV can be both powerfully symbolic and therapeutic to document this pinnacle time of change in your life.

I would suggest unplugging it, then getting some good gloves and goggles and take a sledge hammer and go to town on it. At the very least, put it in storage or cover it with a nice decorative something or other but get it out of your scope of vision and attention. Don't kill your TV only to be on your iPad, laptop, and smartphone 24/7. Life continues just fine without having to check Facebook and Instagram every 15 seconds. It is mind boggling how lives have changed since everyone now walks around with their attention glued to the mini computers in their hands. I have to admit my smart phone plays a part in my daily life but I'll also say it wouldn't be the worst thing to toss the fucking thing in the garbage or give it the sledge hammer treatment. As far as using the smart phones, the less the better. They as does television block and disrupt your potential to raise your frequency of vibration and become truly self aware. They emit harmful Waves of radiation soon to be worsened with the introduction of 5G technology. Do not be fooled, do not listen to the people that say they are harmless. My warning to you is keep them away from your body as much as possible.

Warren Buffet and Bill Gates are friends and both self made multi billionaires. They were simultaneously interviewed separately and asked the question how would you describe the key to your success in one word and the both answered the word being "FOCUS".

If you are truly serious about your success and improvement the "super distractors" of modern living 2019 have to go! It's simply not going to happen with your face buried into Facebook, Youtube, Instagram, Twitch, Fortnite, Netflix, Drinking and Partying with your Buddies ect.

News flash, for you to manifest and build your dreams and aspirations its going to take your dedicated FOCUS. For an experiment I implore you to purge these master distractors from your life for a 2 week period and read some good books, practice meditation, mind power, physical exercise, interactive physical games where you engage with others in a live setting as your only sources of entertainment. I swear the craziest new phenomenon is people/friends getting together and instead of interacting and engaging one another they all got they face stuck onto they fucking smart phones like trained mesmerized monkeys! Just try to go two weeks purged of the fore-mentioned "super distracters"and see after that time if you don't feel like you've just emotionally and physically detoxed off some brainwashing toxic reality like a harsh drug addict kicking heroine.

Step 2. Once the super distracters have been removed from your daily routine or at least god willing weened from suckling the super distracter Teet to a minimum , it's time to start building and assembling your library. Leaders are readers, folks, and there is great power and wisdom to be absorbed through reading books on a daily basis. You might think it a boring endeavour as most people haven't read more than two or three novels since they left high school. But once you give it a try and see how your imagination supplies the mental images with the words you're reading you may find it a very entertaining endeavour. I can tell you new synapses will be fired, and your mind will take a new empowering journey contrary to the hypnotic mind death that TV and its modern day distractor/vibration frequency interrupter cronies supply.

Start with topics and books that spark your interest be it fiction, how to books, biographies or whatever tickles your fancy get started and dive right in. The daily habit of reading will supercharge your ability to manifest the law of attraction this I can promise you. It's a new era so yes e-books are fine but the old school hardcover and paperbacks are best, especially if you're just starting to get back into the practice of reading.

Audio books are also fine and can be handy on your morning commute or at work instead of listening to tunes or negative talk radio.

SKILL 2: GOAL SETTING

Dreams and wishes remain just that until they are articulated and written down in the form of goal setting. A goal broken down into steps becomes a plan. Brian Tracy said, "Goals are the fuel in the furnace of achievement. It is not possible to realize even a fraction of your potential until you have learned how to set and achieve goals as normally and as naturally as you brush your teeth, or comb your hair in the morning." Lots of people might have some idea of what aspirations they have for their life but very few take the time to sit down and think it through charting a path to achieve a set goal and to ask the question if you're willing to pay the price for your success.

You could say that the practice of writing things down successfully achieves the task of simply keeping you on track of what you need to do/accomplish like a grocery list but the truth is there is much more to it than that.

When you put old school pen to paper it brings those goals to life with magical metaphysical power. You are making a binding contract with the infinite intelligence to manifest desires.

This magic does not happen the same when typed out on a laptop or iPad. Written goals are a magical power source, a lasting form of expression that even after you have stopped writing continues to exist.

Once the goals are physically written out, they keep emoting their intention and power emissions while you are doing and thinking other things and keep the spiritual/quantum momentum going until you next come back to focus on them.

- On lined paper write out all the goals that are important to you big and small in the best detail you can.
- Don't write them in the form of I will accomplish this and I want to get this or that done someday.
- Write them out in the form that you already possess what it is you desire to manifest; that you have already accomplished, achieved the task.

Straight outta the book of old-school this is a very ageless and powerful action and not to be overlooked. The universe will give you what you want if you want it badly enough. If you can't take the time to physically write out your goals for what you want then clearly you don't want them that badly. What kind of devotion, dedication and discipline of mindset is needed to ramp up the vibration to transmit to the infinite intelligence with your mind power you might ask.

Imagine having your head dunked under water and two minutes later your soggy head is pulled from under the water gasping and sputtering half drowned. Imagine in the two minutes, especially near the end, how desperately you desired to breathe in some air.

Well, soon as you can train your conscious mind with that kind of all-consuming desire to attain what you want as much as the desire to keep breathing to keep your body alive! That's the level of desire and dedication needed to raise your vibration and link up with the infinite intelligence.

What I'm about to say now is very important and a key factor in empowering the law of attraction.

Napoleon Hill says in *Think and Grow Rich* that you need an all-consuming and burning desire to achieve your goals. And I've just used the example that your desire need be as strong as breathing in a survival situation. The desire must be focused strongly dedicated to faith, desire, imagination, and persistence, yes. But what you must not do is allow feelings of desperation, an unhinged kind of spastic unhealthy wanting mixing with your emotions of what you desire. Have intense desire but have focused calm and measured desire that you can trust the infinite intelligence to deliver on the universal promise.

The same as an animal can sense fear if your wanting is all-consuming and obsessive but unstable and riddled with feelings of desperation. The infinite intelligence will sense it and not respond favourably.

When you set forth to manifest the law of attraction properly, it has no choice but to follow universal law and your commands consistently given from the wheelhouse of your conscious mind to the engine room of your all-powerful subconscious mind. These commands are your investment capital. In the law of attraction as you practice mind power each day, you make them work to make them grow like investments with compound interest with persistence and focus on the things you wish to manifest; when you visualize your desire in your mind it will drive your actions with laser focus.

SKILL 3: GET ORGANIZED
GET DISTRACTION AND CLUTTER FREE

Organizational skills are key to self-improvement.

Cluttered environment = cluttered disorganized life. If you find yourself sitting at your workstation and you take a look around and see a lot of clutter in your environment it's a proven fact that the clutter is a major distraction.

Take a look at the interior of a friend's car or living space. If it is clean, neat, and tidy then the chances are that they live an organized and structured life, and if they are messy and disorganized, filled with garbage and clutter, the chances are that their lives are disorganized and haphazard.

Clutter in your living and work space must be eliminated either organized or perhaps a majority of things altogether tossed out.

Chances are if there is lots of clutter a good portion of it is garbage or useless stuff taking up room that you don't use or need. Toss the garbage items. Give away and store the stuff you don't need. Before you store the stuff you don't need. Identify the stuff that really should be tossed even though you may want to keep them around. Things that hold no significant value other than some hokey sentimental connection like, "Gee I've been keeping this useless garbagy thing around for so long it's like family. How can I toss it now?"

Make an executive decision to toss everything possible and things of some kind of value clothes you never wear trinkets, etc. Give them to the Salvation Army or friends that will take them.

When you define the things that absolutely can't be discarded or gifted away put them in storage. Good old Rubbermaid bins are great for this purpose

Your workspace needs to be organized and clutter free. Also your living, sleeping, and driving (interior of your car space needs to be clutter free). It is a proven scientific fact that clutter in your environment that sits in your field of vision will constantly distract you, whether it's straight up garbage magazines, newspapers, pizza boxes from days ago, empty beer cans, clothes everywhere and other stuff. If this is you, don't feel bad cause in my bachelor days this portrayal was definitely me. The constant clutter, constantly, subliminally distracted as it does and my disorganized life followed suit.

If you have too much clutter the key is after you get organized don't slide back, don't leave stuff in your car that needs be tossed/taken out.

When you arrive home to do a quick clean up and organization so you can stay on top of it, don't rip off your clothes and let them sail onto the couch or wherever, which for me was a favourite pastime. In my case, as with many people, you may need to hire someone once or twice a week to help you stay on top of a clutter-free environment.

Sitting down to a clean desk and work environment that doesn't have pens so old they don't even write and magazines and papers that have no relevance scattered all over the desk surface is not the way.

It's amazing how liberating and empowering a nice clean workspace and living environment can be if it's not what you're used to.

SKILL 4: BE AN ATTENTIVE AND ACTIVE LISTENER
Don't gossip, try to eliminate negative sources and people from your life. Adapt a teachable and open mindset and aggressively seek out mentors and great teachers to learn from both in your field of interest and fields unrelated as you will find highly successful people all possess

coachable skills that are valuable and transferable to many various areas of business and people/team management. You'd be surprised how many highly skillful and successful people are willing to share their life's experiences to help you advance yours.

> Pastor Jeff Hall wrote in *A Winner Knows*, "A winner still knows how much he has to learn even when he is considered an expert by others. A loser wants to be considered an expert by others before he has learned enough to know how little he knows."

People simply don't listen to one another properly anymore. Instead of listening, everyone is focusing on what they are going to say when it's their turn to talk or not even waiting their turn and cutting in talking over people. Attentive listening is a valuable skill and lost art for most.

> "God gave you two ears and one mouth.
> Use them proportionately."
> —Susan Cain

Don't join in at the water cooler chatter or any situation that lends itself to gossip or involving yourself in negative talk about other people you work with. But keep it real. If your team's goaltender crapped the bed and couldn't stop a beach ball the previous night then of course let him have it both barrels, we are all human and taking the 100 percent high road may be admirable but talking about the rookie scoring the team's lone goal, just doesn't cut it, sometimes in good fun we need to vent.

This is especially true if you're a hockey fan in Vancouver where you have to mortgage your house to see a game and maybe throw in a week of overtime ho urs if you want to purchase a beer and hotdog. Yet in 40 plus years of embarrassingly inept mismanagement, the team never has won a cup. The lovable and legendary Pat Quin gets a hall pass on the crosshairs of this accusation of managerial futility due to the fact he was, in my opinion, the greatest hockey man that ever lived, and I love the man and his memory like I do my own grandpa. Even though I never met the man. And to his credit, he got us one game from a cup victory in the '94 NHL cup final with a team he built from scratch as GM and coached himself. Okay, that was admittedly a bit of an off-topic tangent.

Remember!
- Try to eliminate negative energy sources from your life.
- Don't help conflict build in any area of your life.
- Make the peace when you can, and if you can't it's time to walk away.
- Try to oppose "us versus them" thinking.
- Value compassion
- Choose empathy over blame and intolerance.
- Put ego aside in some instances and don't be so obsessed about being right.
- Try to be generous of spirit

When someone else is in trouble, be of assistance, and don't ignore the signs of distress.

Try to be the proud doer of at least one act of unsolicited kindness every day even if it's as simple and effortless as combining a friendly greeting with a smile to a frowning person, melting their frown into a smile. This one is a personal favourite of mine. It converts an unhappy stranger to global sister or brother of unity and love. It works especially well with the grumpy old folks where you can see the years of negative dissatisfied existence literally etched within the lines of their face, of course, some of them may be having none of it and try to take a whack at you with their cane, such is the risk and such is life.

Try to eliminate negative/toxic people from your life. It gets tricky if they are family or friends but if they are a dragging you down, always soaking up your valuable time and energy or routinely presenting drama requiring you being the rescuer. Then surgical removals of them from your day to day inter-people relations are necessary or at the very least quarantined from your inner- to the outermost circles at arm's length. It's better to inform them exactly why you chose such an action so as not to sugar coat the situation and enable them to seek out their next victim.

SKILL 5: DEVELOP PATIENCE AND THE DISCIPLINED RITUAL OF DAILY PRACTICE

It carries 10 times more weight to practice for a short amount of time every day than to practice 12 hours straight six times a month. There is a huge strength in daily practice. Once you get in the zone after 30 to 60 days it will be imprinted to your mind and become habit forming and that much easier to stay in the zone of Daily practice.

Too many people don't have the patience or persistence towards real and lasting change in their lives. They quit too soon after a brief period of being inspired and then sink back into their old daily routines. They throw their hands up and say this whole law of attraction, Mind Power thing is BS "I tried it and it didn't work."

As far as affirmations and meditation go, although results can sometimes come quickly it often takes hundreds to even thousands of times to really start to reprogram the neural pathways of the subconscious mind and manifest desires. The challenge is to stay focused and be disciplined to stay the course and with patience and believe you will get there. It's up to the individual. There's no better time to start than the present. It might take seven years to attain a worthy goal but the fact is the seven years are going to whizz by regardless, so much better to start your plan and make the most of the time you have.

Everybody wants to improve the quality of their lives. This is inherent in all human beings, yet there are very few people who know how to do this. Start observing your own behaviour, and you'll see there's a pattern in your behaviour and that pattern starts when you wake up in the morning. If you kick your alarm clock, you probably find yourself sleeping in a lot of the time. If you're late for meetings and deadlines, you're probably late a lot of the time. These behavioural patterns that we perpetuate are in turn producing the results in our life.

Discipline is really the ability to give ourselves a command and follow through.

Discipline is something most people don't understand, when we were punished as kids we were disciplined. Most people think that discipline is generally a form of punishment. Discipline is really the ability to give ourselves a command and follow through. A disciplined person decides what they're going to do and they discipline themselves to do it. This kind of discipline must be developed into your way of thinking and your life.

Many wannabe mind power practitioners want to jump out and transform into a ninja law of attraction machine, but to get there no one wants to do the sometimes mundane daily practice of basic exercises and the patience to stay the course essential to achieving such a task. It reminds me of what my high school basketball coach said to me when I was practicing my free throw shots, which was not as fun as practicing fancy reverse lay-ups or setting up the springboard they used for gymnastics, getting big air and slam dunking volleyballs like we were NBA stars. My coach said, "Joe, numbers wise, the reality if you want to be a decent free throw shooter at the high school level, (which was Victoria High School at the time) is that you have to first make over 10,000 attempts before you'll have enough repetition to imprint it where you can do it with a reasonable success rate." I remember thinking that number being absurdly high, but I did understand the message of the level of commitment needed towards the pursuit of excellence. But perhaps not as much as two times NBA MVP Steve Nash must have, not far away at St Michael's University School. It's well known that above being a naturally gifted athlete, what got him over the top was his unmatched work ethic to practice and perfecting the small details.

With me, I found making moves and driving to the basket came naturally, and I made some pretty fancy if not risky moves to score to the chagrin of my coach. Making fancy moves and driving to the hoop was the most fun of the game. But learning to work my one on one play and moves into a team game concept with set plays took a lot of work for me. The part of my game that most needed improvement was the jump shot. After school each day I would practice my jump shot religiously until it finally started hitting with more accuracy. Shot after shot going through the motion of keeping your eye on the basket to the point of releasing, the backspin and arc with the end result hopefully being its going swish through the net instead of an air ball. As my shot became more accurate with constant daily practice, I gained more confidence in my shot.

The biggest tool I had was envisioning the shot being successful in the beginning motions seconds prior to the shot attempt, which brings us back to the thinking of already having accomplished the thing it is your desire to come to fruition. Going mentally through my motions and routine as I had done hundreds of times before, I could relax and sit back on that foundation of preparation and just let the shot happen fluidly and naturally. Practicing the shot on an open court it's fairly easy to sink baskets swish after swish in no pressure situations, but when people are running at you trying to bowl you over, knock your ass down and take the ball away, it's a whole new ballgame. That's when in the game situations with the pressure on, my built up foundation of practice was there to have my back.

The great power of good old boring practice is that it builds a wall of repetition that has your back when you need to really focus and deploy with your best accuracy in less than accommodating circumstances. You're in the war zone adrenaline pumping, bombs going off everywhere, yet amongst the intense distraction you can set into your trusted routine, stop time, space and sound, and see only the basket (the task ahead of you). Though the opponent might be frothing at the mouth like a rabid dog howling and hurtling towards you to knock you down and take the foul after the shot you still have your two seconds to jump and release the shot within those milliseconds first envisioning it in your mind the same as you did in practice your eyes to the basket focused you know it's good to go as soon as the ball leaves your hands taking the shot.

" ... persistent daily practice is an all-important method and
a tool toward being able to master the power of imprinting
your subconscious mind."

This is the power of boring repetitive daily practice. Each new day,
of practice combined with the strength of the previous days of practice
building and building momentum to a huge powerful wall of practice.
The important knowledge gained in practice such as what worked
well, what didn't work so well, refining your talent towards whatever it
is you're practicing to reach excellence. Inspired, persistent daily practice is an all-important method and a tool toward being able to master
the power of imprinting your subconscious mind.

We live in a 'get it now get it fast' society and few people have
the patience for imprinting their subconscious minds with the habit
of daily practice. Few people have the patience to trust in the law of
attraction and give it the required amount of time to come to fruition.

During the time that the infinite intelligence sets forth creating what it is you want and desire there is the gestation period of
the manifestation.

During this time, the thing you want is going to ask you every day,
"Are you sure you want me?" It is not for us to say when we get what
we want, it certainly doesn't hurt to set realistic timelines and work
towards their realization. But ultimately, the infinite intelligence knows
exactly when is best for your goals and aspirations to be manifested.
And most all of the time it's going to take some time with serious
challenges along the way.

Sure you might gather all your smartphones, iPads, TV and whatever vibration transmission blockers around your living space and jet-
tison them out the window, achieve perfect mind and body alignment
with a disciplined healthy diet and exercise regimen. And you might
then build a pyramid that is aligned to magnetic north with a crystal
blessed by a Tibetan monk placed under the apex and sit within that
pyramid with a Sri Yantra placed in front of you intensely meditating and focusing on a vision board posted to the wall in front of the
pyramid with a picture of a million dollars the chosen vehicle to which

you can attain your goal and vision of "mental freedom and peace of mind /happiness."

And you might sit there for a week within the pyramid, eat, sleep, drink, only so you can spend every waking moment meditating to the highest rate of vibration within your subconscious mind as is humanly possible to channel the law of attraction. Two weeks go by and you go down to the corner store buying a lottery ticket and that night it's announced you bought the winning ticket and the millions of dollars pictured on your vision board are soon sitting on your coffee table in physical reality. You say to yourself, "Now that's what I call "law of attraction supercharged".

Your wife at the time quickly decides she is better off divorcing you and getting her share of the money which she promptly does. You then marry an even more heartless trophy wife who proceeds to break your heart to little pieces and milk you for as much as she can get all the while you get involved in some extra sketchy business dealings with some extra sketchy characters who milk more of the money. Then in a botched attempt to "do you in" to get the last of the money your jealous and greedy family members blow your right arm off with a shotgun.

To your dismay, you turn to alcohol and drug addiction and five years from the time of your winning you finally piddle away the last of your millions of dollars. At rock bottom, you join a support group get cleaned up and sober, start radically changing your train of consciousness and thought and move to a Tibetan monastery without a penny to your name to live and meditate in a state of "mental freedom, peace of mind, and happiness" and finally attaining your original goal within the timeframe, the universe and infinite intelligence had planned for you from the start.

"Nothing worth anything ever comes easy."

The most dedicated practice of mind power humanly possible is not typically going to drop your desired aspirations on your lap. But, the more you practice, the more time and dedication you put into mind power manifestation, the better your results absolutely but that's because you're proving the strength of your want and your will to the infinite intelligence. Most every time, there will be patience required and an appropriate waiting period that is predestined the moment you set wheels in motion.

Nothing worth anything ever comes easy. We are tested and challenged for the very reason of putting your faith, belief, patience, and persistence to the max of how strongly we want what we want.

The infinite intelligence will test your faith, belief, persistence, and patience to stay focused on what you want even while what you desire is slowly methodically being assembled for you within the train station holding room of desires and aspirations that is the universe of infinite probability/possibilities. Trust that the infinite intelligence is assembling the people, and situations to be presented to you at just the right time for you in just the right circumstances that fit your aspirations perfectly.

In the movie *The Matrix*, our hero Neo starts by elaborately dodging bullets to where in the end when he has mastered the Matrix he simply puts his hand up and stops the bullets in flight as they fall harmlessly to the ground. Pyramids, crystals, and Sri Yantras, etc. are fun tools to assist your quest to master the law of attraction. But once you begin to become self-aware and truly master the art of mind power, you simply won't need them. Every day is an opportunity to increase your Knowledge. Through daily study and practice, you develop an understanding of the principles of mind power, auto-suggestion, visualization, the power of creativity, imagination, persistence, faith, and belief.

CHAPTER 4
DAILY EXERCISES IN THE LAW OF ATTRACTION

Let's get right to it then!

> "Life passes most people by while they are busy making all
> their grand plans for it."
> —Quote from George Jung, character in the movie *Blow* as
> depicted by Johnny Depp.

Don't just wish and dream. Take action! We are all dreamers. Every one of us. Everything that gets created by people in the physical world must first be imagined. But to bring dreams and thoughts to fruition of reality, you must make a plan for that to happen and then follow through on your plan.

> "Wishing will not bring riches. But desiring riches with a
> state of mind that becomes an obsession, then planning
> definite ways to acquire those riches through goal setting
> and backing those plans with a persistence which does not
> recognize failure, will bring you what you desire."
> —Napoleon Hill, *Think and Grow Rich*

Napoleon said it well but to be brutally honest, most people completely suck at this.

If you live an ordinary life all you'll have is ordinary stories. Test yourself, take risks, seek adventure.

The other big and common setback is that people don't realize that if you bitch and complain negatively about how your life sucks then a negative and sucky life is exactly what you will continue to attract to yourself. My point being is that the power of your subconscious mind is always at work whether you want to use your conscious mind to get actively involved and steer the ship or not. Whatever you really want, you will get. And whatever you really don't want, you will also get because these things, good or bad, are what your subconscious mind is primarily focused on

To those people that are always complaining that they can't catch a break and that their luck is shit due to a bad childhood, etc. Here's a tip:

Shut your yap, quit feeling sorry for yourself, put on your big girl/ boy pants on, read through this book, use the information provided in this book and let's get on with it. The past is done. It's time to create a new exciting future! I'm not trying to be insensitive to the fact bad and crippling things do happen to people. There is always going to be others better off then you and others worse off. What we witness all to often is the lazy ass sense of entitlement for little or no sincere effort, whining and complaining. And you just want to walk up and shoot these people in the knee cap or transport their ass to some third world country to walk five miles for clean drinking water. And pronounce "there you go now you have a legit reason to bitch".

Here's the thing about when you're chewing your friend's ear off, going on and on about your problems and lack of luck. Fifty per cent of them nod their head sympathetically while they think about something else because they could care less and the other fifty per cent are thinking they're glad it's you instead of them. Ok, that might sound a bit cynical. Perhaps a few people will genuinely listen and care like good old Mom but for the most part folks, this is the deal.

Start cultivating your action plan to get what you want but know here's the mistake most people make when they're making plans. They make plans that something will show up in a certain way and then they go about doing the things that are necessary for those plans to become a reality but they block out the possibility that the idea's going to show up in a way that they hadn't planned in an unforeseen way. Generally speaking this is what happens when you're doing what you're doing in the order that you believe is necessary for something to show up sometimes it shows up from another unanticipated direction. You must learn to trust that the infinite intelligence knows much better than you and will get you to the finish line but more often than not in a completely different fashion than you originally planned.

In 2003, a woman I was dating at the time said, "Joe, you're ambitious and got some great ideas but you're too scattered. You need to focus," and she handed me a copy of the book that would change my life, *Think and Grow Rich*.

I read along with an open mind finding it quite interesting and came to the section where it said, I'm going to tell you exactly how, in the pages ahead, to realize your dreams but only five per cent of the people reading this will actually try it out. I read that and thought, *Well I'm going to follow the instructions and be that much farther ahead than the other 95% of idiots that don't.* I read the following pages where he introduced a six-step process that I thought was amazingly innovative and cool. But, it was five years later before I gave it a try. Just like the other 95% action less fools that I said I wouldn't be.

I'm saying to you don't be part of the fool club. Life is short. Start now! I'm not appealing to the people who will read this book more for the entertainment value and do nothing, though I appreciate your buying my book. The law of averages suggests there will be many. Just as there will be many that will get short-term inspiration but still again ultimately do nothing.

I appeal to you, dear reader; the one who is going to take action and use these powerful principles to live an extraordinary life and make a difference. I applaud you. Get excited! Dive right into it. Become it and make exciting things happen in your life. Stay the course and practice every day. I can't stress enough how daily practice is required and habit-forming, in a very good way. The breakthrough moment will come. It will slap you across the face as a real self-manifested miracle. At this moment, you will fall to your knees in a quivering mess, pee your pants and scream up to the heavens, "Good Lord Jesus, this shit is for real! And you will know in that moment everything will change for you!

Disclaimer: the quivering and dropping to your knees, pee your pants part, will vary from person to person. Such an epiphany will strengthen your belief as you become inspired to move mountains. At least 15 minutes twice a day, I would say, is the minimum requirement. The more you can do, of course, the more benefit you will get.

Repeated visualization and meditation is very effective for channeling your subconscious mind to create and manifest your dreams and aspirations. Create a burning desire and spark a passion to attain goals that excite you to think about. Obsessively, but also confidently, imagine the end objective every day as much as possible. You can then trick your subconscious mind into accepting the visualization as a part of reality, and it will start moving mountains to manifest those very same visualizations.

In this chapter, I would like to introduce an exercise so you can test drive the possibilities of channeling the power of your subconscious mind. I call it The Law of Attraction Action Plan (LOAAP). Basically, it entails the practice of writing out your goals, posting them up, and reading/speaking them aloud each day, in the morning and before bed. Writing your plan out physically and speaking it out loud is very important. It helps program and empower your subconscious mind to attract what your desire. 95 to 97 people out 100 will either say that its complete nonsense and a waist of time or say perhaps theres something to it but couldn't be bothered to try. Im telling you there is a very real power to speaking out loud to the universe exactly what you want and how you intend to get it.

In working out your action plan, try to map out the best plan that you can. If your plan needs specialized knowledge to attain your goals, educate yourself. Study people who have achieved similar successes. Don't be afraid to modify and change your plan as you go. Keep focused on the end result more than the specific way you're going to get there. What you think is a perfect way now may completely change by the time you actually reach the top of the mountain. Chances are they will. With that being said, don't keep making changes on a whim. Make smart, calculated, well thought-out, researched plans.

> "Your achievement can be no greater than your plans are sound".
> —Napoleon Hill, *Think and Grow Rich*

When creating and adopting a plan don't fall in love with your plan so much that you're unwilling to change and modify the plan if events dictate that you should.

When making plans, keep these facts in mind:

Think it through. Try to foresee potential pitfalls. Try to map out your plan as bulletproof as possible taking into account shit does happen and no plan will be entirely faultless.

Seek the council of talented people and utilize the experience, education, and imagination of their minds. You can only accomplish so much on your own. Utilize a team of people working towards a common goal/vision. This use of the mastermind principle is a very powerful tool.

If what you really want seems completely unattainable for your current life circumstances don't sweat it. As long as you stay the course with belief, persistence, and a burning desire for its achievement, the opportunities will present themselves. Be alert. Identify the opportunities when they present themselves, and, act on them immediately. Once you start on your journey and do the daily meditation and affirmations and practice of mind power, you must become pliable to the ways of the quantum field and listen to the hints and gentle nudge and whispers in the wind that will help guide your way. The universe can sometimes be tricky and the very best opportunities to guide you towards a course of action may be right under your nose as a subtle clue. The infinite intelligence/superconscious mind likes to play with us in this way. Do you need a great idea to get started? Your subconscious mind will supply it as a thought, or perhaps someone will walk up and drop it right in your lap. It can actually work that magically.

As far as the goals you set, don't be afraid to think big and aim for the sky. Big dreams are awesome! I say, *hell yeah!* Don't limit your ambitions in any way. Bob Proctor says if he has an idea that scares him a bit, and all his friends and associates say that's crazy, it'll never work, then he knows he has a great idea. The thing about dreaming big is that you must convince yourself to believe in your heart that it can be real. As you read it, think it, speak it out loud daily. You can speak out affirmations and your master plan verbally at the top of your lungs to the universe until you're blue in the face, and out of breath, but if you don't sell yourself and believe it in your own heart, it will never happen.

Here is a DEAL BREAKER ALERT! To empower the subconscious mind you have to convince your conscious mind into believing it can be so. This is the key to its success and why so many try the Law of Attraction and fail to master it.

You must master the Law of Belief! The Law of Belief will empower your dreams and aspirations to come true. Your subconscious mind is a principle. You must know what the power of belief is, why it works, and how it works.

The law of belief says that whatever you hold within your thoughts long enough, maintaining the belief that they are true, will eventually become your reality. Whatever you subconsciously feel to be true from the world within long enough will ultimately manifest in your world without.

What we believe and confidently expect in life, we receive – simple but true. We only raise ourselves as high as our believing takes us. This applies in every realm of life: physical, mental, material, and spiritual.

And again if your main goal is a big one as , break it down to smaller achievable and realistic actions that can build confidence and help propel you towards your ultimate goal.

Don't have too many dance partners, which is to say, don't try to tackle a bunch of things at once, so that no one thing gets enough of your focus and attention to be successful. By all means, brainstorm and write out all your good ideas. Find the one that you are most passionate about and move forward with that single goal. Don't worry if at the outset that it seems impossible, because again, I will tell you the universe, the superconscious mind, will introduce what is needed at exactly the right times for you.

All will be explained throughout the course of the book but for now, as mentioned earlier. Let's get right to it with LOAAP. The Law of Attraction Action Plan.

I want you to start your first draft of LOAAP right away. We will go through the techniques that will supercharge the process in your favour and guide you how to best modify or change your plan. But first, let us dive right in and imprint your subconscious mind with the habit of practicing the law of attraction/mind power on a daily basis.

To start, you need to assemble lots of pens and lined paper notebooks. It's very important that things are written out as opposed to typing them out on your tablet, iPad, or laptop. There is a special magic that takes place when you do your goal setting with old school pen and paper. It's good to back up and keep records of your plans on your PC or tablet/iPad, but first and foremost write everything out with pen and paper. This is essential and must not be skipped.

LOAAP

When creating your law of attraction action plan at its most basic elements, here are the steps:

Step 1: Know what you want. Pick a goal that you are truly passionate about and enjoy doing.

Step 2: Believe in your success, write down how your quest might change your life and the world in the process.

Step 3: Become passionate, present (live it every day) and positive.

Step 4: Write down specific goals that are part of your vision.

Step 5: Write down the action steps that need to be taken to accomplish your goals.

Step 6: Rank your action steps from most important to least important.

Step 7: Get in the game, commence your ass kicking take no prisoners mission. Don't wait till your action plan is perfect and polished. Get out there and get your feet wet. Shit happens, and there's no perfect plan. Roll with punches and bumps on the road and adapt as you go.

After defining your ultimate goal, pick a 3-month, a 6-month, and a one-year short-term goal, as stepping stones towards your ultimate goal and aspirations.

For example, it could be mastering a musical instrument, producing a number of art pieces, increasing sales at your work, or excelling within the organization where you are employed, etc. These are examples of attainable short-term goals that once achieved, add confidence and belief in the process. These ultimate goals could be becoming an international success in music or in the arts. Or mastering the ins and outs of the business/organization you're employed by, so you can ultimately become the owner of your own business/organization.

It's very important to have a good vision of your ultimate goal before choosing your short-term goals so that they are in alignment. Draw upon your imagination and follow your passion for faith and belief. Don't worry if your goal seems too far out of sight. The universe will magically present things, people, situations, and circumstances along your inspiring journey to help and guide you.

Ok, so let's say you've brainstormed what it is in life that will make you truly happy. What for you is a worthy long-term goal that you can truly be passionate about and what as a starting point could be some short-term goals to set out and accomplish towards the fulfillment of your ultimate goal?

On a piece of lined paper first, write out your long-term LOAAP and then write out two or three (or as many as you like) short-term LOAAPs.

LONG-TERM LOAAP

Step #1

Write out the long-term goal and a timeline for when you want to accomplish the goal. It's very important when writing out the goal to not write it in terms of 'I will' or 'I want to' accomplish such and such. You must write it like you already have what you want to achieve.

Example

Wrong: I want to be the owner of the most successful commercial real estate firm on the west coast. I will achieve this task by the summer of 2022.

Right: I am so happy and grateful now that I own the most successful commercial real estate firm on the west coast. I have attained my goal within the timeline of 2019 to 2022.

Step #2

Determine exactly what you intend to do and what you plan to give yourself in return for accomplishing the goal. The quantity and quality of service you render are how your success will be measured. Write it out, once again omitting any use of the words I will or I want to. It is best to come up with your own, but feel free to use my example if you like. It's the one I first used.

Wrong: I will work tirelessly; daily with full intent, determination, passion, imagination, burning desire, faith, and belief in myself to bring my goal to fruition.

Right: I attain my goals by working tirelessly every day with full intent, determination, passion, imagination, burning desire, faith, and belief in myself.

Step #3

Write out your plan of action to attain the goal.

Wrong: I will acquire the specialized knowledge needed. I will learn every facet of the business. I will seek out and learn from the most successful leaders in the field of the commercial real estate. I will assemble a mastermind team of talented hand-picked individuals working in harmony with me towards the attainment of my goal.

Right: I am acquiring the specialized knowledge needed. I am learning every facet of the business. I seek out and learn from the most successful leaders in the field of commercial real estate. I am assembling a mastermind team of talented hand-picked individuals working in harmony with myself towards the attainment of my goal.

SHORT-TERM LOAAP

Step #1

On lined paper, write out steps 1 through 3 above for your short-term goals that complement your ultimate goal.

Example

Short term goal #1 – Success at sales in commercial real estate

Step #1

Write down the short-term goal and a timeline for when you want to accomplish the goal.

Wrong: I will, I want to be the top salesperson at my work, selling the commercial real estate. I want to increase my sales quota by 70% by December of this year.

Right: I am so happy and grateful now that I have achieved top sales at my place of work, selling commercial real estate and increasing my sales quota by 70% within the year.

Step #2

Determine exactly what you intend to do and what you plan to commit of yourself in return for accomplishing the goal.

Wrong: I will work tirelessly; daily with full intent, determination, passion, imagination, burning desire, faith, and belief in myself to bring my goal to fruition.

Right: I attain my goal by working tirelessly; every day with full-intent, determination, passion, imagination, burning desire, faith, and belief in myself.

Step #3
Write out your plan of action to attain the goal.

Wrong: I will acquire the specialized knowledge needed. I will take courses on the best sales techniques and practices. I will learn from people who have mastered the art of sales in my chosen field of commercial real estate.

Right: I'm acquiring the specialized knowledge needed. I am educating myself on the best sales techniques and practices. I am learning from people who have mastered the art of sales in my chosen field of the commercial real estate.

Short term goal #2 - Enroll and complete a business course in commercial real estate.

Step #1
Write down the short-term goal and a timeline for when you want to accomplish the goal.

Wrong: I will take and complete a course in business management for the commercial real estate by the end of summer.

Right: I am actively involved in successfully completing a course in business management for commercial real estate.

Step #2
Determine exactly what you intend to do and commit of yourself in return for accomplishing the goal.

Wrong: I will work tirelessly; daily with full intent, determination, passion, imagination, burning desire, faith, and belief in myself to bring my goal to fruition.

Right: I attain my goal by working tirelessly; every day with full intent, determination, passion, imagination, burning desire, faith, and belief in myself.

Step #3
Write out your plan of action to attain the goal.

Wrong: I will hire one-on-one tutors, and I will make sure to set aside extra hours for further study in the field of business management for commercial real estate. During these times, I will store away my television so that I am not distracted. I will keep my living and work space clutter free. I will keep a positive mindset and maintain a healthy diet combined with physical exercise to keep my mind and body in alignment for peak performance.

Right: I'm engaged with one-on-one tutoring. I manage my days so that I spend extra hours towards study in the field of business management for commercial real estate. My television is history, and thus, no longer a distraction. I keep my work and living space organized and clutter free. I keep a positive mindset and maintain a healthy diet combined with physical exercise to keep my mind and body in alignment for peak performance.

Now choose your favorite written short-term goal and complete steps 4 through 7 of LOAAP.

But first, take your other written short-term goals and your written long-term goal and put them in a binder. Or if you like, post them on a vision board in the vicinity of your workstation. Cut out and paste some cool and inspiring images and affirmations around your written goals on your vision board.

Step #4
Take your written statement and tape it to your bathroom mirror. Read it aloud twice every day: before you brush your teeth, morning

and night. Read your statement out loud while you look yourself in the eyes, with confidence and total belief, envisioning that you have attained the goal and accomplished your mission.

Step #5

Write out your goal, in a condensed version, on a card that you can put in your wallet or purse. Keep it with you every day. Take out the card and read it twice a day during your morning and afternoon break. Or, at the very least once a day during your lunch break. On one side, write out your goal. On the other side, write this excerpt from Matthew 7:7-8, the Sermon on the Mount. "Ask, and it shall be given you; seek, and ye shall find; knock and it shall be opened unto you: For every one that asketh receiveth; and he that seeketh, findeth; and to him that knocketh it shall be opened."

This little gem comes from *The Strangest Secret*. Don't get all bent out of shape that I'm going all bible thumper on your ass. Just follow the instructions. Keep the card with you at all times. When you're out and about, believe that the biblical words written on the back of the card are fulfilling a prophecy for your life. When you take the card out and read it, believe magical power is at work.

Step #6 – The Gratitude Foot Wiggle

Last, but not least, every morning from the first moment you open your eyes, think of something in your life that you're grateful for and wiggle your feet while you do it. Do this before you hop out of bed. Mix up the things you're grateful for, but, do it every day and make it a ritual habit. Also, do not skip the foot wiggle for this daily exercise or you're missing out on the full benefit of the exercise.

This practice, as you continue mastery of mind power, can evolve to become a ritual morning meditation. But for now, this is a quick and easy starter and you would be amazed how this one small action can positively affect the rest of your day.

As the book goes on, I will introduce practices and exercises and information that can supercharge the process, as well as explain why and how things work the way they do. Get started right away and give it a good try. This is exactly what Earl Nightingale said in *The Strangest Secret* 60 years ago. He said, "Give it 30 days. If you drop off start again and do a full 30-day cycle." Now, he didn't say 30 days because that is just enough time to become a millionaire with the new daily mantra of affirmations, and written goals. I too will say, try LOAAP for 30 days while you continue to read the book, and if you drop off start again and do a full 30-day cycle. The reason being, it takes 30 days to develop a habit. It's then easier to keep doing it. You don't need to know the principles behind what I'm asking you to do right away. Just trust me and do it. Do it and I promise you, you'll already be ahead of the 95% of other people that read through these principles by whichever source, and took no action.

Throughout the process, it is imperative that you keep an open mind and be willing to learn and be teachable. After you've completed the first 30 days, continue to do these practices for 60 to 90 days to make actual imprints within your subconscious mind. Ultimately, keep going, day after day and never stop. Become a lifetime student of mind power and the law of attraction. The learning and the empowerment of the learning is truly never-ending.

By the same token, you could use the Law of Attraction for evil. But, going down that path of revenge, or selfish, immoral gains will inevitably end in your undoing. The very same negative power you embrace will inescapably consume you and destroy you from the inside out.

The power of love excludes selfishness and embraces sharing and selflessness. It embraces having heartfelt gratitude for all the good things in your life and guides you to think in your endeavours to increase your wealth and quality of life. You can be of service to others less fortunate and give back, while still advancing yourself. Ditch the hate, ditch negative habits, actions, and ways of thinking, and go with love to guide you whichever path you choose. My brothers and sisters it's not just the good way, it's the only way.

If you find yourself losing it on someone and bitch slapping them upside the head for pissing you off, I won't sugar coat the fact total loss of composure and physical assault of another is not just wrong but mildly psychotic behaviour. That said shit happens it's not the end of the world. Apologize, forgive yourself, correct and continue. Tomorrow is a brand new day mofo.

CHAPTER 5

IT'S MEDITATION TIME, YO!

INHALE...   EXHALE...   FUCK IT!

The Art of Meditation is an immensely powerful tool for the manifestation of your goals. It can be practiced by anyone, anyplace, and it doesn't cost a dime. It is extremely beneficial and can help us to feel happier. There are many types of meditation and various different folks practice it for a multitude of different reasons.

I promised to introduce techniques to supercharge the process of mind power. I can tell you now, the single best way to become centred and tap into source energy so as to channel your subconscious mind, to manifest what you want and supercharge the law of attraction, is the practice of daily meditation. It can accelerate your manifestation ability and bring your mind and body to the right place to magnetize your desires faster. If there is anyone habit you embrace throughout the course of reading this book, it should be the practice of daily meditation. Meditation has the power to eradicate the harmful paradigms engrained in your subconscious mind and release you from the Matrix. Meditation allows you to reset your mind to serenity and clarity. Meditation gives your mind a break and a most needed a restful retreat from the constant buzz and stress of modern living. To practice meditation, you don't have to spend hours sitting in the lotus position. You don't have to be a Buddhist, Hindu, or follower of any religion.

Meditation's origins come from the Eastern countries such as India, China, and Tibet where it's been practiced for over 5,000 years. It goes hand in hand with traditional Eastern religions, such as Hinduism and Buddhism, where different types of meditation are used as a means to get closer to God. Not nearly enough people in North America meditate but it is increasingly growing in popularity. There is a danger in this though, where the practice of meditation can be minimized and not properly respected. It is important to know that although it is relatively easy to learn and practice, it was never created to be a mass-marketed self-fulfillment tool.

Meditation was conceived in the Eastern countries as a long-term discipline, a lifelong practice. Spiritually rich and not easily mastered, it's easy to jump in and effectively learn and benefit from meditation as a beginner, which is the beauty of meditation in that it is both simple and basic but also deep and complex. To explain further, I tell the story of my wise karate teacher when I was young. He showed me a number of kicks in one session. He told me though the moves were basic enough, to master them could take a lifetime.

Meditation was never meant to be commercialized and represented as a fast acting super med like Ativan as it can be in Western culture. Wise people know meditation needs to command a gracious level of respect.

Let's look at some of the most popular forms of meditation.

1. TRANSCENDENTAL MEDITATION (TM)

Transcendental meditation is a very simple technique. It is not because it's simplistic practice or a meditation for beginners. But instead, because there is a very heartfelt , earnest and elegant simplicity to the practice of transcendental meditation. It is a natural process without suggestion or manipulation of thought.

There is no black belt level for this meditation. There is no focused concentration or controlling of the mind. In contrast to other meditations it is basically effortless – easy peasy. Everyone can practice it just as well as anyone else. It's simple to learn, and the benefits can be felt immediately.

TM is not a meditation for the masses that you learn through Google, recordings, or a book. It is always taught one on one by a trained and certified teacher of TM. It is taught over consecutive days for approximately an hour to an hour and a half each day.

It can be practiced 20 to 30 minutes every day sitting comfortably in a chair with your eyes closed, and it can be done just about anywhere you are at any time where you can be comfortable at peace and close your eyes.

It is not a mantra-based meditation in that its main focus is directed towards transcending to your peaceful inner self but it does involve the use of mantras. You sit quietly in a comfortable position, close your eyes, and repeat a mantra. Through this meditation, the goal is to transcend your ordinary thinking process to a state of pure consciousness, dissolving mental boundaries to a state of tranquillity and perfect stillness.

What TM is not is it is not a philosophy. It doesn't involve any change in lifestyle daily routine or diet. It has no connection to any particular religion or belief. To understand how TM compares to other meditations? Imagine yourself out in a boat and large swells are all around you. You think, *Holy crap, the whole ocean is in storm mode.* But in reality looking at the whole ocean on top there are these gigantic waves but they are minuscule compared to the depth and immensity of the ocean. No matter how crazy things are on the surface of the ocean. No matter how high and violent the waves, most of the ocean's natural state is silent and mellow. That is its basic nature: active on the surface and silent within. The conscious mind is the active and thinking mind; it is our surface mind. All the things we concern ourselves with during our daily doings are like the waves crashing about on the ocean surface. With all the craziness in daily life, especially nowadays, there is a natural wanting for some inner calm, clarity, peace, inspiration, and happiness.

Broadly speaking, this benefit can come from all meditations but is certainly the case with TM and more easily accessed compared to some other meditations. The operative word here is inner. And just like the large body of the ocean below the waves exists, your subconscious mind is an immense and powerful source of peace, tranquility, and happiness.

Throughout the book, it may seem I constantly give the subconscious mind this rock star status compared to our custodian small player conscious mind but really the conscious mind is just as important and most importantly is how they sync together for both meditation and your daily thought processing. No matter whether you're losing your shit going ballistic, there is a level of your mind where calmness exists. This is where your source of unbounded creativity and power of manifestation exists. It's all powerful and it's always there waiting for you to simply access it.

In a nutshell, transcendental meditation is the natural and simple technique to transfer yourself from the hectic crashing waves of the surface of your mind – your active thinking conscious mind – to the serene and calm depths within. The unified source of consciousness, which is your subconscious mind, is infinitely linked to the superconscious mind/infinite intelligence. You're not creating this calmness, you are simply accessing what is already there and always there within the deep recesses of your mind.

How do you know you've achieved this process when practicing transcendental meditation?

During TM, the goal is to effortlessly calm down your mind to quieter levels. Done properly, you can reach a level of calm and relaxation superior to your deepest state of REM (rapid eye movement) sleep. When we are in a state of stress and anxiety our adrenal glands secrete cortisol. When we secrete cortisol we feel more anxious, which can be a vicious circle. Scientific studies show TM, as well as other meditation techniques, can drastically reduce cortisol levels, increasing serotonin levels the happiness neural transmitter and an increase in the hormone called prolactin, which is connected to the feeling of well-being.

Within the state of calm and relaxation is your opportunity to release and dissolve feelings of stress, fatigue, and tension.

In life, your mind has a natural tendency to be drawn towards the most satisfying option. You're in a room and classical music is on the radio boring the hell out of you but you can hear Iron Maiden playing in the room next door so you go next door to listen to the Iron Maiden or if you're an old fart you go to listen to the classical music that you hear next door or if you're really a young millennial as I'm dating myself with the Iron Maiden reference you might hear some Dubstep DJ music coming from another room and be drawn towards that. My point is the natural tendency for the human mind to be spontaneously drawn towards something more satisfying. The same as we are naturally drawn to things in our outer world, the practice is to draw yourself within to the more satisfying calmness and serenity within.

Same as you teach a child how to dive: simply stand before the water, lean forward, cup and point your hands, and the rest happens naturally and easily. When we train ourselves to draw to within the calmness of our subconscious mind, our body naturally follows as they react as one in the same.

2. HEART RHYTHM MEDITATION

Heart rhythm meditation begins with posture. Start by sitting in a chair upright feet flat on the floor with your spine straight, shoulders back, look straight ahead neither down or up. This posture produces immediate calm and peacefulness. This is called 'the monolithic position' because you sit in a chair like a pharaoh. This form of meditation focusses primarily on the heart with an emphasis on observing the characteristics of your breathing.

Your spine, like an antenna, is a superconductor that radiates the energy from your heart. You observe the characteristics of your breathing: the length, the depths, and the direction through your nose to your mouth.

This rhythm that is coordinated between your breasts with the heartbeat creates a rhythmic coherence in a state of balance through heart and body. As stated elsewhere in this book the heart is the most powerful magnetic and electrically charged organ in your body. By linking to your heart chakra through meditation you can activate your core self. And your heart and your heart's desire is the connecting point between your conscience and subconscious mind. What is in your heart is what you will experience in life. If you look there with humility and honesty, you can find your purpose in life.

3. KUNDALINI

Kundalini meditation originates from both Buddhist and Hindu practices. Its translation in Sanskrit is "coiled". Kundalini is a healing energy that is said to lie dormant at the base of the spine in the sacrum bone. Through meditation, it can be awakened. The kundalini is connected directly to human awareness and infinite intelligence. Through the enlightenment and self-realization gained through meditation, you can awaken the kundalini in the process of balancing the other chakras, concentrating on breathing as it flows to throughout the energy centres of your body. Becoming clear, awakened, and enlightened through meditation you can attain a new clarity and vision of life; you can see everything from a completely different dimension. Fundamentally, successful kundalini meditation is to move towards a higher plane of perception; to transform from a limited physical perception to a higher awareness of endless possibilities.

Kundalini meditation gains more power and benefits the more you do it. Twice daily is recommended.

4. GUIDED VISUALIZATION

Guided visualization is a newer form of meditation. It can be used for personal development, spiritual healing, and stress relief. It follows along the law of attraction for its manifestation theme in that the emphasis is on the defining vision of your aspiration or desire. Guided visualization can tap into the subconscious mind by using your imagination to focus the direction in a proactive way. This meditation is not just a mental meditation. It involves your entire body, your emotions, and your senses. Guided imagery visualization is one of the easier meditations for most as it requires less time and discipline to develop a high level of skill. That's because your mind and imagination are naturally ready to drink in the appealing sensory images. You can create your own imagery within your imagination or listen to imagery that has been created for you.

5. QIGONG

Qigong is one of the oldest forms of meditation and is a branch of traditional Chinese medicine. There is acupuncture and herbal medicines and you have Qigong. There are trained practitioners who can manipulate the Chi by moving their hands over a person's body. Chi is your life force, your vital energy, as well as all the energy in the universe, and the term chi gong means to cultivate your vital energy/ life force.

Theoretically speaking, when the body is in a state of slow and relaxed movement you may use the mind to lead the Chi into the deeper places of the body's energy centres. It is a favourite because this meditation improves respiration and posture and promotes relaxation. It involves movement and focused breathing techniques to circulate throughout the body and its energy centres. In Qigong practice it is very important to master the trick of correct breathing. It is in the exhalation that leads to the five centres: the head, the centre of both palms, and two centred points on the sole of both feet. Adulation also leads chi to the skin where it is exchanged with your surrounding environment. Inhalation leads Chi deep within your body to the organs and marrow. Chi is in everything and in the practice of Qigong meditation you are working with your own personal chi to build it up and make it stronger to live a longer, happier, more fulfilled life.

There are different types of Qigong meditation and possibly hundreds of different methods.

6. ZANZEN

Zanzen meditation is one of the purest forms of mindfulness meditation. It is a very simple yet precise method of meditation with an emphasis on the correct posture. Stability in the body creates stability in the body. Zazen translates to "seated meditation". It represents the heart of Zen Buddhist practice. Like the previously mentioned meditations, breathing is an essential element. It is an easy meditation to engage in because it relies on self-guidance.

However, it is more difficult to master and progress due to the lack of guidance.

7. MINDFULNESS

For last, I have left the most popular and practiced meditation in Western culture, that being the practice of mindful meditation. It is derived from a 2,500-year-old Buddhist practice called Vipassana or Insight Meditation. The Buddhist term "Sati" translates to "mindfulness".

Mindfulness is a quality that everybody already has, but most people have not been advised they have it and it can be cultivated. Not only is mindfulness something we all naturally possess, but it becomes more readily available to us when we practice on a daily basis. Whenever we bring awareness to what we are directly experiencing via our thoughts and emotions, we are being mindful.

How do we use meditation to channel the Law of Attraction, you may ask? Through meditation we want to transmit energy vibration with our subconscious mind. Energy is always in movement. Energy has always existed and always will exist. With meditation, we can propel energy to attract what we focus on.

You should meditate every day for 5–10 minutes to start. Try to do it for 30 days consecutively, to establish the habit of doing it. Pick a time that you can set aside every day when you will not be interrupted by anyone or anything. For many people, it's first thing in the morning. Or if you're not too tired, just before bed. In this five to 10 minutes each day, the idea is to completely detach yourself from the world. Most importantly, get started and start feeling the many benefits of daily meditation. You will start to feel less stressed out. Small things that used to annoy you will no longer have the same effect. Your health will improve and your concentration and energy levels will be higher than ever. As you get more and more skilled at meditation, so will it increase your mind power to manifest the abundance you desire. So let's get right to it, shall we? It's time to meditate, yo!

Energy is always in movement. Energy has always existed
and always will exist. With meditation, we can propel
energy to attract what we focus on.

Let's start with a short and introductory beginner's exercise in mindfulness meditation.

Let's start by sitting comfortably. Try to keep your back straight, not arched. Now close your eyes and concentrate solely on your breathing. See if there is a place that you notice your breathing most distinctly. Maybe it's your nose, chest, or belly. Choose that place where the experience of breathing is strongest for you. You can bring your focus there and just rest. Take smooth and easy breaths focusing in on each breath as you go. As you breathe, images, sounds, sensations, and/or emotions that arise will not be strong if you are properly focused on your breathing. While staying connected to the feeling of your breathing, let thoughts effortlessly flow by. Understand the idea of meditation is to quiet our minds; to focus our attention inwardly and pay attention to the present moment, without judgment.

Mindful Meditation is the act of release, not shutting down.

Mindful Meditation is the act of release, not shutting down. Think of your mind as a running stream. Trying to shut down your mind from wandering into thought is like trying to stop the running stream from flowing with your bare hands. The idea with meditation is to step out of the stream, and let your thoughts flow by effortlessly.

Focus on your breathing with the understanding that thoughts will come and go as they please. There is no stopping them or controlling them including thoughts such as, *what am I going to have for dinner tonight? My car needs repair, Becky's tuna surprise sure gave me the farts*, etc. The goal is to focus your mind enough on the breathing that the thoughts flow by as you maintain focus. If a moment comes where a thought is strong enough to interrupt and pull you away from your focus on breathing, stop, and return your focus on breathing and begin again. The most important moment is in the moment after a strong distracting thought pops up and disrupts your focus. This is the place where you practice letting go. You must let go of the distracting thought and begin again. Focusing on your breath until another distracting thought pops up. Let that thought go too and start again. Do this again and again. Don't feel like you're failing or doing it wrong. We are predisposed and conditioned to be distracted and to stray. Each distraction is an opportunity to practice letting go and starting over. Each interruption and restart is like a bicep curl for your brain.

Let thoughts flow as they will. Let thoughts say whatever they want. If a negative thought pops up, you don't need to get rid of it or fix it. You simply need to let it flow by. Keep coming back to your breathing and the present moment. Beginners, when first trying this technique, may find that zero thoughts are flowing by and every thought is disruptive. Here is a little trick, while relaxed and focusing on your breathing think these words to yourself, repeating the mantra: *my breathing, my breathing, my breathing* over and over to help block out any interrupting thoughts. This action is like training wheels. The thoughts still come but the mind chant keeps your focus on your breathing enough to more easily let them flow by. Soon, as you find you can go for a minute or more, take away the training wheels. Stop the mind chant, and try to fly solo, for as many breaths possible before a stronger disruptive thought pops up.

This simple act of quieting your mind and focusing on your breathing is a rebel against the grain of normalcy that few people in North America make the time and effort to embrace. You are breaking a lifetime habit of walking around in a fog of mental autopilot and conditioned rumination, to stop and become present and whole with, the right now. There is profound tranquility and discovery to be found in the present moment. It is immensely more important than moments past that have come and gone and the future that is yet to be. We have 50 to 70 thousand unconscious thoughts per day, of which 80 per cent are unfortunately negative. When meditating, you don't know what your next thought will be. Will it be about the future? Or the past? Will it be a question or an answer? A judgement or a comment?

There is profound tranquility and discovery to be found in
the present moment.

There is no, I did bad or good when attention goes to thoughts
because you have no control over it. In the Western world, our minds
are preprogrammed to think certain ways. We have thoughts that state,
it's bad to look this way, or good to look that way. It's bad to have this
job, and good to have that job. It's bad to rent an apartment and good
to own a home. It's bad to be single and good to be married, etc. etc.
You're using the same preconditioned matrix mind to try and meditate, so of course, it will come with the self-imposed inner turmoil and
judgement that you need to release.

Example:
It's bad to have negative thoughts. It's good to have positive thoughts.
It's good to have a quiet mind. It's bad to have a busy mind.
It's good to give attention to the present. It's bad to give a lot of
attention to the past and future.

Forget about all of that!! Thoughts come and thoughts go. That's it.
And that's the beauty of mindfulness meditation. Don't try to fix or
control anything. Stop and let each moment be exactly as it will be.
Don't think, I need to get from my current experience of mega mind
chatter to this wonderful experience where my mind becomes silent
and quiet. This way of thinking is a trap. Peace and freedom come from
recognizing that no experience is bad, wrong, insufficient or lacking.
Meditation is not a tool to get you from a bad experience to a good
experience. Don't judge your current experience. Let it be and go
along for the ride. Lose the anxiety of what experience you might be
trying to control or achieve. Stop and let the experience be exactly
what it is. Stop and let yourself be as you are. Stop and be with yourself.

Ok, so we start with mindfulness meditation to quiet our mind and
become present at the moment with source energy letting thoughts
flow by without judgement or overthinking.

Now we can practice methods to channel our energy and raise our frequency of vibration to align ourselves with the life experiences we seek and desire.

The term meditation means to become familiar with.

The term meditation means to become familiar with. Through the use of meditation, we can get into the operating system of the subconscious and begin to make measurable changes. In your quest to disconnect from the matrix of paradigms, you need to become consciously familiar, aware of your unconscious thoughts, your unconscious habits, and your unconscious emotions.

Mindfulness is a state of creative potential. The common mistake is that people believe the transformation to enlightenment is uncommonly hard and only achieved by Tibetan monks after a lifetime of study and practice. How do we define the state of enlightenment? Let's call it the highest state of fulfillment.

Your state of consciousness shifts as you reach new stages of personal change.

It's all standard issue to every human brain waiting for our embrace understanding and expression. People spend most of their time ruled over by their primal state of stress function based on fight or flight, and these stress responses spring up from our minds a pre-programmed/conditioned paranoia and insecurity because in each instance we are not actually experiencing any real potential threat.

Remind yourself of the reality that there is no threat and that self-awareness/enlightenment alone is enough to reduce many kinds of stress reactions and find a higher balance. The

purpose of meditation is not only to become aware of the old self thoughts, behaviours and emotions but to become familiar with a new self and begin to ask yourself during meditation what is the most ideal version of myself and the person you aspire to become. Visualize leaving all the negatives of your old self and embracing all the positive qualities of the new self. As you force yourself into new mental territory and begin to think differently than you normally think, you're forcing your brain to fire new synapses in new sequences and combinations. When you're doing this you are rewiring the workings of your mind. As you make your brain fire in new ways the nerve cells become rewired in new ways as the scientific term for this reprogramming process is the use of neural plasticity.

> When you're immersed in a meditation and you are dreaming, you're rehearsing a new reality of being.

The advantage and fun of being a human being is that we can make thoughts more real than anything else; we do it all the time. When you're immersed in visualized meditation and you are dreaming, you're rehearsing a new reality of being. If you're truly focussed and truly paying attention there will come a moment when your conscious mind becomes so activated, so awake the thought that you're thinking about will literally become the experience. The end product of the experience is human emotion.

Your unconscious subjective mind does not know the difference between the actual event that produces the experience and the thoughts that you're having. I will repeat this concept often as it is critically important to understand. The body, which is one and the same with the unconscious mind, doesn't know the difference as you modify the emotional environment and the body/subconscious mind begins to change. Through the practice of daily meditation, you can reproduce that same emotional state every single day and begin to condition your subconscious mind to no longer living in the emotions of the past. With your mind and body working together you come to a new state of being. If you can become familiar with this new state of being then you are no longer living in a reality that is connected to the old stuff and you steer your direction to a new destiny.

Unfortunately, most people wait for a personal crisis/drama or loss to get going about the process of change. They wait till the ego has been knocked to its knees to its lowest denominator until they finally say I can't go on living like this in this life the same way and they begin to inspect their own way of thinking. They begin to pay attention to their behaviours and ask is this really loving to me; is this really healthy for me? They notice the emotions they been holding on to that have been connected to experiences from years and years ago. No sense in waiting for crisis as your call for action – seize the moment and take action now.

At some point, you need to come to terms with the old self and the negative, self-sabotaging matrix programming you've been conditioned and subjected to so why to wait till a point of crisis? You can start now! You can awkwardly try to learn and change in the state of suffering or you can easily and fluidly learn and change in the state of inspiration.

Get truthful with yourself to know yourself through meditation. Become so conscious of these matrix programs that they don't slip by unnoticed. When you're truly in a creative state is when you forget about you. Make it your goal to connect to universal source energy and become present in the moment. Not just when you're meditating but conditioning yourself to live in a state of mindfulness in your daily living, hiking in nature or immersed in painting a work of art, or walking the seawall, or taking a golf swing. Moments you completely disconnect with your ego self and your personal identity is when energy moves from those survival emotional centres in the body and moves up to the heart. At the moment it moves to the heart, you start to feel inspired.

In meditation, a person can become completely detached from ego consciousness and become selfless to forget your body, your identity, the people you know, the places they go, the things they have to do, or the things they own to become no one, to become nothing.

You channel your mind and thoughts to go nowhere. Forget about your appointments in the past. They become no time and that is the moment you become conscious. That is the moment you begin to disconnect from the biology of who you are. When you manipulate your mind and body to a state of pure consciousness, you can begin to change your body. Only when you are beyond your body, can you heal your body and create some new experience in your life, create some new future event in some future time. You have to get beyond predictable linear time.

If you're going to create some new experience in your life, some new event in your future by thought alone then you have to become thought alone and that is the moment when you become pure consciousness when you are nobody, no one, nothing, nowhere, and in no time. That is the moment that you are no longer constrained by your preconditioned matrix reality. This is the moment that your free-willed subjective human consciousness merges with the quantum field and the objective universal consciousness and it is at this juncture when they merge together you come back to awareness.

Each time you mentally chill and go there, you take a piece of it with you and you become more like it, you become more willful to become more mindful; you become more conscious, you become more loving, become more giving, its nature becomes your nature.

Learning how to achieve this through meditation is powerful and potentially life changing.

CHAPTER 6

HEALTHY BODY ... HEALTHY MIND. THE IMPORTANCE OF MIND AND BODY ALIGNMENT FOR COMMANDING THE LAW OF ATTRACTION

Your body and mind are the instruments to implement mind power. As your body goes, so does your mind. Therefore, it makes sense to practice mind and body alignment for peak body and mind performance; to enable your subconscious mind to transmit with the highest frequency rate of vibration possible.

Harmful vices like alcoholism, smoking, drug addiction, and prescription drug dependence are among the usual suspects for wreaking havoc on your body and mind. This wrecking crew of destructive addictions, whichever one you may be afflicted by, is the ball and chain from which you must release yourself. Until you reach deep inside, channel all your strength, and break through that wall, you will be forever stuck at ground zero. We all know people who have struggled with these issues or ourselves have struggled or are struggling.

In modern life, alcohol and drugs can be a very popular escape not to mention that high school mentality that it's what edgy and cool people do at parties. The zippy and fun dabbling in recreational drugs can quickly turn into an ugly overwhelming addiction that sends your life, bank account, and relationships straight down the toilet. There are deep seated emotional reasons connected to people's various addictions and that's exactly why they can be so hard to kick. Unfortunately, many people wait till they hit rock bottom before they reach out for help. The professional help is out there, and some of the best help and guidance comes from former addicts who can relate to a hell of addiction.

Smoking is the act of poisoning yourself many times on a daily basis. They might taste great with coffee or a cocktail but folks if you can muster the strength, they gotta go for more reasons than I can list. Cigarettes contain more than 4,000 chemicals, many of them cancer-causing, but at the top of that list I can tell you they directly interfere with your rate of vibration to manifest mind power in a most negative way

Ok, so let's say you feel you are fairly vice free with a fairly average lifestyle. Well, unfortunately, the trend for most people these days in North America is that the "average" are overfed, under-exercised, under hydrated, over drugged and sleep deprived. To be the maximum you, and feel good to face each day, it's a quick no-brainer that you want to be eating right, engaged in daily exercise, properly hydrated, not reliant on the popular prescription drugs and properly rested with a full night's sleep.

There are four main areas for proper body maintenance. They are:
- **Proper sleep**
- **Healthy diet**
- **Proper hydration**
- **Daily exercise**

1. PROPER SLEEP

Studies show people are sleeping less than they did in the past and sleep quality has decreased as well. Everyone knows sleep is beneficial, but the healing and repairing benefit impact on your waking hours through proper sleep is highly underestimated.

Lack of sleep can be ruining. A person can survive longer without food than they can without sleep. Proper sleep is vital to your health and emotional well-being

Sleep plays a vital role in promoting physical health, longevity, and emotional well-being. It is essential to your immune system, metabolism, and all vital bodily functions.

You simply cannot achieve optimal health without taking care of your sleep. For peak mental performance, your body needs 7–9 hours of regular nightly sleep. With at least one hour before midnight (2–3 hours is better) if possible. Try to sleep and rise at approximately the same time every day.

Take an objective look at your sleep environment. How effectively do the blinds block the light? How is the room temperature? And most importantly, make sure your pillows and mattress are just as they need to be for your individual needs. Some people do better with hard mattresses and some people swear by memory foam. Everyone's likes differ, but, make sure you're not sleeping on a shitty old mattress that no longer gives the proper support and needs to be replaced.

2. HEALTHY DIET

Here is some wisdom and universal truth biscuits: We become what we think about, and we are what we eat.

To give your body the proper nutrients needed each day, a healthy eating plan is required. Be responsible for not consuming too much junk/unhealthy foods and be good to your ticker. A healthy eating plan lowers your risk of heart disease.

When thinking about what consists of a healthy diet think in terms of what a caveman had access to back in the day as in real food as opposed to processed phoney imposter food. Natural living food is properly digested but the fake, unnatural dead food is not properly digested. Everything that does not come from mother nature is extremely difficult for your body to digest and eliminate, it sticks to the walls of our intestines and forms a toxic waste coating that in turn gets toxically delivered to our blood stream and every cell in our body. Try to completely eliminate dead unnatural processed fake food from your diet. Think whole grains, fruits, vegetables, lean meats, fish, poultry, eggs, and nuts. If you like dairy, go for low-fat dairy products.

Try to control portion sizes. Perhaps eating more times a day to stay full as opposed to skipping breakfast only to pig out the rest of the day. Processed foods have a lot of saturated and trans fats, sodium, and added sugars, which are to be avoided.

Back in the day when the caveman couldn't access the supermarket, food was the real thing. Nowadays, there is far too much toxic crap in the food we consume. The phrase "processed food" doesn't sound healthy and that's because it absolutely is not.

Some of the ingredients added to processed foods are borderline poisonous: high fructose corn syrup, vegetable oils that are hydrogenated transforming them into trans fats and other additive atrocities that you can hardly pronounce. Canned food, dehydrated food, chemically added food is all processed food and makes up over half the average North American diet.

When vegetable oils like palm, soybean or corn are obliterated with hydrogen and turned solid they become trans fats. Trans fat is an antinutrient and adding it to packaged foods, the supermarkets can store them on shelves for an eternity without having to worry about them going stale or rotting.

Refined grains are to be avoided, the very worst of these being high fructose corn syrup (HFCS). Embrace the whole grains like wild or brown rice, and whole wheat bread.

HFCS is in practically everything. It contains dangerous chemicals and contaminants and should be purged from your diet. It is sweeter and cheaper than regular sugar and it's in every processed food and sugar-sweetened drink. If you want to have some sugar, go ahead have a little sugar or honey, but add it to your food yourself. Avoid eating food with added sugar. Check labels and try to cut HFCS out of your diet completely.

All artificial sweeteners are crap and to be avoided. Aspartame, Saccharin, and Sucralose————> All crap. Check labels. Don't ingest them. They are linked to hypertension and cardiovascular disease, increasing your risk of stroke, heart disease, and other diseases

Benzene is a proven carcinogen, avoid the preservatives sodium benzoate and potassium benzoate.

Avoid Sodium Nitrates. They are used in processed meats, like jerky, bacon, luncheon meats, and hot dogs. They are believed to damage your blood vessels causing your arteries to narrow and harden leading to heart disease

The beef industry introduction of meat producers fattening up their cattle with hormones for quick to market beef as well as to increase their milk production has affected our diets.

Eating a natural real food diet of the least toxicity possible makes the best sense. Don't trust that we are told we can't ingest enough pesticides or additives to do us harm over a lifetime. We most certainly can and you should always wash your fruits and vegetables at home before consumption.

Stress in our daily lives is another factor that can negatively affect our body and mind alignment. These are the invisible toxins that we are exposed to that degrade our well-being such as depression, major stress, physical, or emotional abuse. You can't see or taste these invisible toxins but they are equally destructive to your physical health and well-being.

That's the toxic crap you don't want to consume or be exposed to. Now let's look at some beneficial foods that you should eat every day.

Blueberries:
Blueberries are rich in anthocyanin, a flavonoid with potent antioxidant capacity that can help prevent a host of maladies.

Garlic:
Garlic has antibacterial and antiviral properties. According to 22 studies synthesized in the book *The Immune Advantage*, just six or more cloves of garlic a week can "slash" your risk of stomach, colorectal, and prostate cancer in half.

Olive Oil:
The benefit of olive oil is that it lowers "bad" low-density lipoprotein (LDL) cholesterol and raises "good" high-density lipoproteins (HDL)

cholesterol. Olive oil is also packed with antioxidants called phenols, which may protect artery walls from cholesterol buildup.

Broccoli:

As Dana Carvey will tell you, you gotta have your broccoli so get chopping up that broccoli. Broccoli consumption can boost production of enzymes that detoxify potentially cancer-causing compounds. It can also decrease your risk of everything from lung and breast cancer to colon and stomach cancer.

Yogurt:

Yogurt contains nutrients key to maintaining bone health and contains live beneficial bacteria, known as probiotics. Probiotics lessen the growth of harmful bacteria in your gut.

Oats:

Eating cooked oatmeal or oat bran can lower your blood cholesterol levels significantly and reduce the risk of heart attack.

Flaxseed:

Flaxseed is revered for its lignans and fibre, the omega 3 fatty acid ALA shown to have many potential health benefits. It can help reduce cortisol levels, which is a stress hormone.

Green Tea:

It might well be the healthiest beverage on the planet. A very powerful antioxidant, green tea can protect against the buildup of "bad" LDL cholesterol. Forget an apple a day. People who drink a cup or two of green tea a day have a significantly lower risk of developing narrowed arteries and a host of other health benefits such as improved brain function and a lower risk of cancers.

Beans:
Beans are awesome food for your heart. They contain soluble fibre, which soaks up cholesterol so the body can repel it before it can stick to artery walls.

It all really comes down to common sense. We know that raw and natural foods are good for us and the drive-thru processed phony food is crap/toxic food. Statistics show millions of people are consuming the crap food. So try to be aware and consume the crap in moderation or eliminate it from your diet completely. Make healthy choices like skipping the drive-thru and cook healthy meals at home and prepare healthy lunches you can take to work each day.

3. PROPER HYDRATION

So many people underestimate the importance of proper hydration for the body and mind. If you are not optimally hydrated, every moment of each day, then you can't transmit with your subconscious mind at maximum vibration. Your brain, your blood, your lungs, are all predominantly water, and our entire body is over 60 per cent water.

Water is critical to the balance of all the body's systems, including the brain, heart, lungs, kidneys, and muscles. Drinking water regularly helps for healthier teeth, skin, joints, and bones. It promotes better digestion, absorption, circulation, and maintenance of body temperature.

Staying optimally hydrated is key to optimal health. Far too many if not most people don't drink enough water and are not properly hydrated. Walking around with bodies being not properly lubed with water is like an engine low on oil: our parts slow down and grind up.

Most of us are dehydrated without even knowing it. Without proper hydration, your body cells get congested. Your skin can't detox. And your bladder and kidneys won't work properly. You'll feel tired and lethargic.

Remember to opt for pure, clean, filtered water whenever possible. Don't ever consider sweet juices, tea, or worst of all coffee or pop as substitutes for pure water. They don't hydrate you nearly as well. Sugar, salt, and caffeine dehydrate the body. Try to make changes like lose the morning coffee ritual. If you can't, at least drink a tall glass of water to counterbalance the dehydrating coffee. It is said the average adult should drink eight 8-ounce glasses of water a day for optimal hydration.

4. EXERCISE DAILY

The human race evolved from nomadic ancestors; they spent most of their time on the go, hunting for food and shelter and traveling miles and miles on a daily basis. Our bodies are evolved through time to be regularly active. Daily exercise is important to increase energy levels, improve muscle strength, maintain a healthy weight, and increase brain function. It's good for your heart, lowers your risk of developing Type 2 Diabetes, enhances your immune system, reduces the risk of certain cancers, and can improve your sleep and a general sense of well-being. Everyone faces different challenges as far as how much daily exercise they can do and the intensity. What we know for sure is that laziness and obesity in North America have reached epidemic proportions.

If you don't typically exercise a lot and are now willing to commit to daily exercise, make a conscious effort to exercise as much as you can. Start gently, at first, so as not to freak your body out. Take walks around the block. Take the stairs instead of the escalator.

Do stretching every day, if possible, especially if you're just beginning a workout/exercise regimen. A minimum of three times per week is needed to achieve benefits.

Once you're in the groove, aim for at least 150 minutes per week of moderate-intensity exercise plus 75 minutes per week of vigorous exercise. It's best to mix up the two in each workout.

Examples of moderate intensity exercise include:
Dancing
Brisk walking
Slow cycling
Swimming
Volleyball
Golf (without a cart)

Examples of high-intensity exercise include:
Running
Skipping/jump rope
Power aerobics
Cycling aggressively
Aerobics
Power walking
Competitive sports
Rowing

Remember, any activity that gets you moving, gives you pleasure, and good feeling gets your heart rate up and racing is a good thing, do it regularly. It's beneficial to you in almost every way.

CHAPTER 7
GET HAPPY. FORGIVE EVERYBODY. BE GRATEFUL. EMBRACE THE POWER OF LOVE. START GIVING

GET HAPPY!

"There is no way to happiness, happiness is the way."
—Thich Nhat Hanh

"When I was 5 years old, my mother always told me that happiness was the key to life. When I went to school, they asked me what I wanted to be when I grew up. I wrote down, happy. They told me that I didn't understand the assignment. And I told them, they didn't understand life."
—John Lennon

Ask the average person on the street what they want in life. Although they might not be able to articulate their plan for happiness or just what it is that will bring them happiness, their answer is happiness. So, what is this feeling of happiness we are all chasing and waiting for? Is it a state of mind? Or, is it an emotion?

Aristotle, the ancient Greek philosopher, believed that happiness was more than a state of mind. You could feel happy, but, you could also be happy. Aristotle thought this was the result when two key elements of our lives joined together: *Hedonia*, the feeling of pleasure, and

Eudaimonia having a good life. Basically being in a good place in life, content, and comfortable brings you to a state of mind that is positive, which reciprocates with more enjoyment and manifestation of an awesome life

Any discussion on happiness centres a lot on dopamine. Dopamine is a chemical in the brain called a neurotransmitter. It is responsible for feelings of pleasure and happiness. The electrical impulses come down the nerves. They hit the connection. The connection releases chemicals. The chemicals diffuse to the next nerve cell. They bind to receptors in the next nerve cell. And they cause an electrical chain. The chemical release is called a neurotransmitter. As we age, from teenage years onwards, we slowly lose dopamine synapses and neurons in our brain. Thus, the use it or lose it theory can apply to our brains as we age. We want to seek out experiences that release dopamine. One surefire way to attain this is through physical activity and meditation.

As far as happiness and the Law of Attraction are related, folks, being happy in the moment is not just a worthy goal. It is the KEY to your future success utilizing mind power. When thinking of your goals and aspirations you must envision them like they have already manifested and get a happy and excited feeling while thinking about them. When I first read that I could have whatever I want if I just asked the universe with belief and desire, my response was, "Great! I'll have a black Lamborghini, a shit ton of money, and a never-ending supply of hot chicks knocking down my door."

Many people are driven by greed for money and material things. Many people have these things and are miserable though. This is not to say that money is bad and those that have lots of it are morally compromised. Money can be a very good thing when used properly.

As I got older and read authors like Wayne Dyer and Louise Hayes, I came to the realization that life is a very short gift. It's at that time that my perspective turned from more selfish gains and materialistic goals to that of a more spiritualistic view, where living an abundant fulfilling life has less to do with acquiring riches and things and more to do with being of service to others and maintaining a feeling of peace and happiness in my heart and mind.

To explain this perspective further, there are two main kinds of goals/values, which people will incorporate into their lives to experience the happiness they seek. Intrinsic goals (being of service to others) and extrinsic goals (Lamborghini and chicks). Extrinsic goals are extrinsic in that they focus on happenings external to you. They focus on rewards, praise, and getting stuff.

The three main extrinsic goals are:
1. Money/Financial success
2. Image/Looking good
3. Status/Popularity

In contrast, we have intrinsic goals. They are satisfying in the way that they cater to an inherent physiological need that is present in all people.

The three main intrinsic goals are:
1. Personal growth – Trying to manifest and become who you really are
2. Human closeness, connected, nurturing, loving relationships – Friends and loved ones
3. Community Feeling – A sense of wanting to make a difference and strive towards improving things locally and globally.

Intrinsic goals are on the exact opposite side of value systems compared to extrinsic goals. They are in opposition to each other. Studies show that the people who are more concerned about having the external stuff like money and status do not typically find acquiring these things brings them the experience of happiness and satisfaction, i.e., money doesn't buy you happiness. These people are more susceptible to bouts with depression. In their day-to-day life, they often find themselves in a void of empty feeling. On the other hand, people who focus on intrinsic goals get fed by the nurturing experiences that fill your soul. They are less depressed and much happier folks.

So many people desire material riches, but don't realize if you are most of the time happy, smiling, content and enjoying your life each day, you are already richer then some of the most affluent/wealthiest people on the planet. Napoleon Hill said, "You need a burning desire for what you want and an obsession for its attainment." But most importantly, when you are thinking and planning the good things you want in life, you have to be happy in the moments that you do the thinking and planning, to have those dreams and aspirations come to fruition. If you're unhappy and feeling negative while you're wishing and goal setting, relying on the thought that once you finally get the things you want, you will then be happy, it doesn't work that way. As Earnest Nightingale said in *The Strangest Secret*, it's like saying, first give me fire and then I shall supply the wood.

The awesome reality is that you can get the feeling of being happy and fulfilled, embracing the power of love right now and be spiritually rich … right now! The irony is when you get in that mindset, your mindset does not change that much with the introduction of financial success and the acquisition of things to your life. As a matter of fact, the less you sweat it out in a state of desperate/unstable wanting, and switch to a calmer more confident reassured approach with absolute certainty and belief in the things you desire to become your reality, the easier these things will come to you. Think to yourself that whatever you want, wants you. Whatever it is that you desire most, is moving quickly towards you.

Happiness is not just about feeling content. More blissful happy people tend to function better when they're more productive. They're healthier and the research suggests they even live longer.

> Here's another tip "don't let shit get you down." One of the key ingredients for happiness is being able to recover quickly from bad happenings.

It's not like happy people don't respond to adversity, we are all human. Their advantage is that they recover more quickly. When shit gets you down don't let it consume and fester. Sometimes, depending on the situation, it's easier said than done to not let bad shit get you down but that's where a daily ritual of striving to immerse yourself with a positive outlook and feeling that things will work out and that even out of the worst things there can be the silver lining. When life steps up and punches you in the stomach the best thing you can do is go within and fix yourself from within through mind power and meditation.

FORGIVE EVERYBODY

How can we further supercharge the practice of employing The Law of Attraction? Forgive everybody!

Why do you need to forgive everybody? Think of all the people throughout your life that you feel have cheated, betrayed, physically harmed, or done you wrong in some way. Chances are, many of those people at this point don't give their past incursions towards you a second thought. But, in contrast, you might be holding on to feelings of anger, bitterness, or revenge. Through the act of forgiveness, you can release yourself from your self-imposed prison of holding negative soul-eating grudges. Powerful negative feelings are screwing you now far more than whatever these people did to you in the past. The act of forgiveness is not so much for their benefit as it is for yours. Forgiveness of others is, in fact, a gift that you give yourself.

A lot of negative thoughts can get piled up and suppressed within our minds. The state is so destroying it might be wise to probe into our own self and note the effect our emotions have upon physical organisms and to forsake every emotional tug that has a debilitating and disturbing effect.

Forgiveness means letting go completely, to abandon. Many people wander around with great feelings of guilt, which is a very destructive emotion. To completely let negative feelings go is a very healthy concept. We have to learn to forgive ourselves. We've got to learn to forgive others. We have to realize that what we did yesterday we cannot change.

You can't hold bad thoughts in your mind and move in a good direction. Form the habit of letting go of anything and everything that is causing you to feel bad.

Having the courage to lose your ego and forgive involves great inner strength. "The weak can never forgive. Forgiveness is the attribute of the strong." —Mahatma Gandhi

Here are some more wise and profound quotes from great minds on forgiveness:

> "Forgiveness is the most powerful thing that you can do for your physiology and your spirituality. Yet, it remains one of the least attractive things to us, largely because our egos rule so unequivocally. To forgive is somehow associated with saying that it is all right, that we accept the evil deed. But this is not forgiveness. Forgiveness means that you fill yourself with love and you radiate that love outward and refuse to hang on to the venom or hatred that was engendered by the behaviours that caused the wounds."
> —Wayne Dyer

> "We must develop and maintain the capacity to forgive. He who is devoid of the power to forgive is devoid of the power to love. There is some good in the worst of us and some evil in the best of us. When we discover this, we are less prone to hate our enemies."
> —Martin Luther King, Jr.

> "If you let go a little you will have a little peace; if you let go a lot you will have a lot of peace; if you let go completely you will have complete peace."
> —Ajahn Chah

In cases where there lies some real deep-set resentment, it can be helpful to write out a letter to the person in question. Be it a former friend, lover, business partner, or family member, explain how you forgive them and why. When you send off the letter, take a deep breath and as you release the letter exhale slowly while visualizing all the negative energy and drama you had put yourself through to that point. It is now being released from your entire being and off it goes with the letter, extinguished from your life/psyche forever. For the best healing results, I recommend the old school pen and paper letter. But, an email or text can work also. Just don't forget to do the exhale and visualization of the negative energy leaving you when you hit Send.

When going through your list of people to forgive, there needs to be one person at the top of the list. And that's you! Your first act of forgiveness must be to forgive yourself for any wrongdoing that you feel you've done to yourself or others. And again, if it helps to write a letter of apology to yourself (I'm serious) or the person that was the recipient of your wrongdoing, then do so.

BE GRATEFUL

As I described in the "Morning Toe Wiggle Gratitude Exercise" the practice of gratitude is the practice of awesomeness.

Through the action of being grateful and expressing gratitude, we can achieve a state of Grace. Through gratitude we become Grace personified. By embracing a mentality of true grace, we embrace the expression of Divine Love. Grace can be described as the amount of light in our soul. The Law of Attraction and the power of infinite intelligence loves grateful people. When looking at superchargers for mind power and commanding the Law of attraction the daily expression of a true heart connected to gratitude is near the top of the list. Feeling and expressing gratitude each day for the multitude of things in our lives for which we can be grateful for can be life-changing. When we embrace feelings of gratitude, it opens up a space of light in every experience. It opens up the light and the path for Grace to flow.

The more we attract things the more we need to be grateful for what we already have – the people around us and life itself. The more we are grateful for what we already have, the more we attract abundance. You will attract this amazing energy and force when you focus on all the things you need in the future. If you are becoming anxious, worried, and tense, remember to become present and focus on the now.

Keep a journal and try to every day write five things you are grateful for. When we experience challenges in our lives that dominate our thinking, business, or health problems, a shortage of money, etc., it is a natural tendency to focus on the problem. However, by doing that, it adds energy to the problem and the problem grows. A mental adjustment of this thinking is needed, and when you introduce thoughts of gratitude you are shifting your focus from the bad to align with attracting good. See what you do want, and don't spend any time thinking about what you don't want.

When you feel overwhelmed, stop yourself and think of the things you're grateful for and make that mental adjustment. Embracing immersing yourself a state of grace is not just about the things in your life that you can be grateful for but to daily embrace a feeling of gratitude for achieving your defined definite purpose before you actually achieve it, this is a mega-powerful Law of attraction tool. Developing a mindset that mirrors the thinking, feeling, and emotions of already having achieved your highest ideals. Play a trick on your subconscious mind and supercharge it into action.

Learn to be grateful in advance for having that which you passionately desire to manifest in your life and you alternately become a lot more attractive. Gratitude is the magic key you start the process with the intention to create the vision and attach profound desire and passion for it to become part of your life then become what you need to become in order to have what you want to have. When you're grateful for already having it before you have it, your conscious thinking mind is going to resist this process, and it's going to come up with all kinds of excuses as to why you can't be grateful yet because it hasn't shown up on the radar yet, but the trick is to actually be grateful in advance for already having something, which you are holding as an ideal. Create the ideal, hold the ideal, attach passionate desire to having the ideal and being able to do things that will help that ideal become manifest. Convince yourself to become grateful for already having that which you hold as an ideal. This is the greatest trick you can play on your subconscious mind. Your subconscious mind becomes a firm believer in the fact that you already have what you aspire, it gets confused by the fact it is not yet in your life and as a consequence it does everything in its power to make that come true for you.

Tap into and trust the universal source energy...

Don't ever make the mistake of saying tomorrow it's going to happen or next month it's going to happen, or next year or when I do a certain number of things this will show up and I will then be grateful. You must shift your consciousness to believe you already have what you desire to attain and be heartfelt and grateful now for already having it. You hold it and you will then become a magnetic powerful attractor to draw what it is that you need into your life. The people, the resources, the financial situation, the tools and technology – whatever it is that you need will start to show up.

And the more things you attract towards your task, the more powerful the attraction magnetism becomes, and the more attractive you become. The more attractive you become once you become a magnet for the creation of what you want to become, the more powerful the magnetism as the things you want start to materialize in your life and add power to your quest.

Tap into and trust the universal source energy to allow for infinite potential reality to provide a mechanism whereby your ideals manifests. You, of course, need to do things. You can't sit around and wait for it to happen. You can't have just passion and desire alone. There must be action and a commitment to your aspirations and the infinite intelligence will respond to your commitment. You need to do the doing, plan and take action. If you do not do the doing the universe does not believe you are committed to your ideas.

Gratitude is the magic key, then the process of forming your intentions and envisioning your ideals attaching to your passionate desire to have them manifest become all that you need to be in every way: mentally, emotionally, physically, and spiritually. You can be all that you're capable of becoming, with the ability to perform at maximum potential and make plans and start on acting on those plans with an expectation of success. Above all, be grateful for already having what you desire to achieve.

EMBRACE THE POWER OF LOVE

> "When the power of love overcomes the love of power the world will know peace. Love is the greatest power on earth. It conquers all things."
> —Jimi Hendrix

There is great power in mind projection and daily affirmations and mediations yes, but it is the power of love that is far and above the greatest power on earth. It is this author's humble opinion that the power of love is what this world is most lacking and needs a hell of a lot more of. Your aspirations are best aligned and will bring you the most happiness if they are embraced and enhanced with the power of love.

Through gratitude we achieve grace. By achieving the experience of grace we become love. The greatest power that exists in our world is the power of love. The power of love is pure, decent, innocent, and true.

> "Three things will last forever – faith, hope and love, and the greatest of these is love." —Corinthians 13:13

Let's look at the different kinds of love.

There is love for your pets, love for your country, love for family members, and love for your partner/soulmate and then, of course, there is the love of yourself. So many people find this last one the hardest: the simple task of loving ourselves the way we are. We are all fragile wanting human beings. Almost all of us crave validation, acceptance, recognition, and acknowledgment from others. Instead of finding the love from within we seek it from others in the form of their praise or approval. Have the courage and faith to trust yourself and immerse yourself with self-love.

The lack of self-love among people is rampant. It's not embarrassing to admit if you don't properly have love for yourself. This is why so many people, including myself, when aspiring to do something bold or potentially great, hit the wall of thinking we are not good or deserving enough to ever achieve such aspirations. And there's usually lots of folks around you to re-affirm the negative assumptions that you need to give up your dreams and fall back in line with the rest of the sheep. Baa baa.

Self–love, at its deepest root, is self-acceptance of who you are. Just as you are. Within all of us is some good and some bad. The whole kit and caboodle of what is you. As Whitney Houston sang in the 90s, "Learning to love yourself. It is the greatest love of all." Corny maybe, but it's *so true*. Until you can love yourself you are road blocked from being able to have sincere love for anyone or anything else. Understand we have nothing to prove. We need only be true to ourselves. The source of love within us is an endless source of strength and empowerment. It is both limitless and timeless. Love is who we are at our core state of being. Insecurity and unsureness are all rooted in fear.

To embrace love and grace within ourselves and our life is the path to self-awareness and living in full powerful vibration. As we learn to practice and become aligned in this way with the life force energy there is no limit to the possibilities the sky is truly the limit. People mistakenly think you have to be a zen guru to tap into the living reality of pure self-awareness but this is not the case. At every moment that you are living and breathing you are immersed with universal source energy. the difference is the people who can spiritually and physically open themselves to embrace it.

START GIVING

One very powerful tool to get the things you want in life is to get in the practice of being a giver. This doesn't mean just money or things as you can very effectively give of yourself and your time by doing charity work and being involved with your community to help people less fortunate. You could volunteer time at animal shelters or soup kitchens, etc. If it's money or possessions you give, give wisely; don't be scammed and give what you can afford to give, don't make yourself broke. Consider everything and circumstances within reason, but if someone reaches out and asks for help you should try your best to be of help. That doesn't mean enabling a drug addict by giving them money since that would actually hurt them but help them emotionally or give them food, sustenance. When giving you must live with the mindset that you expect nothing in return. The universe will give back to you.

Giving is literally like making a deposit in the bank of the law of attraction to be paid back with compound interest.

> Major Law of Attraction supercharger ALERT! To get and start receiving the things you want, become a relentless giver.

Chapter 8
The Superchargers of the Law of Attraction

Desire

The electrical power plant doesn't have the energy, it generates the energy. We don't have the motivation, we generate motivation. A primary driver that will spark your motivation is ambition, the desire for something more. Most people's ambition is set too low because of one time they're disappointed or not supported they fear ridicule, criticism, or potential failure.

> "Dream as if you'll live forever. Live as if you'll die today."
> —James Dean

Ever wonder why some pro athletes lose a major competition even when they are heavily favoured and superior to the victorious opponent? It's the very same reason why you can't achieve a goal you've set out for yourself. The difference maker in the equation is that of desire.

You've heard the stories of the mom lifting the car off her child; of people up against impossible odds but still, finding a way to survive. Unbending will and desire to preserve their life or the life of a loved one is the key. Strong will and desire are the powerful human emotions that can turn the tide and be the difference maker.

We need to understand why it is we want to achieve certain goals and what drives us. This is how we identify our true desire. In life, behind every action, is the motivating power of desire. Every action good or bad stems from desire. First comes a clear mental image of what you want then comes the desire.

Let us explore the expansion of consciousness as it relates to desires and intentions.

Some people believe in the mindset of the 'go with the flow' plan of action whereas others believe that hard work and careful planning are the keys to success. In fact, the best course of action to succeed merges both perspectives together moving forward.

The higher your vibration frequency and self-awareness the better you are connected to universal source energy. In this way, consciousness brings its own fulfillment. The mechanics of desire and intentions will naturally find the easiest and best path to fulfilment. You just need to have the patience and trust that this is so and don't get in the way of it. The more you succumb to your want to interfere and paddle upstream against the natural flow and current the less likely you will succeed in your wants and aspirations

This is to say you must trust and believe in the process and don't try to control the process so much. You must believe and let it flow and manifest naturally on its own timeline. You must let go of your Matrix programming and preconditioned negative thinking. Release the paradigms engrained within your consciousness. Step aside, get out of the way, and let your all powerful subconscious mind do its thing. Let it do what it is magically capable of and was created for, which is to link up with the infinite intelligence and become in harmony with the universe – the quantum field of existence – and start manifesting what you genuinely desire and visualize in your heart, mind, and soul.

The mental image must always precede the material form. Visualization of what you want is key each and every day as the mental pictures and details will become clearer and clearer to you. Visualize the manifestation of your desire and imprint that vision to your heart, mind and soul – live, breathe, and believe it.

Desire needs to merge with a confident expectancy that you will attain your desire. Desire and demand what you want just as you demand and desire to breathe. Think thoughtfully about what you desire and be sure this is what you want; that its fruition will improve your life and lift you spiritually. At every turn, the thing you want is asking do you really want me, thus the saying "be careful what you wish for because you may well receive it". The fact is as you increase your desire and visualization of what you want, that which you want begins to assemble and start moving towards you.

Know what you want and create a fixed idea clearly in your mind. Demand what you want with a confidence, trust, and understanding that the infinite intelligence is real and is busy at work assembling the people, things, and circumstances needed to bring your aspirations to fruition.

FAITH/HOPE

Part of life is there's going to be so many struggles, disappointments, challenges, setbacks, and dark days. Part of sustaining and making it through all of that is maintaining faith and hope. Faith and hope isn't just something that is an airy concept, it is a psychological need to believe that we cannot only withstand trial and tribulation but that we can overcome and succeed, live our dreams, and make a difference.

Hope isn't something that you actually have or lose. We don't have hope, we generate hope. We don't have happiness, we generate happiness. We don't have sadness or fatigue and negative feelings. We generate them. The very thoughts we feed our psyche generate the emotions were feeling.

When your phone is dying you plug it in to charge it up. When your hope is dying you plug it in to charge it up. Happiness, positive energy, and enthusiasm – when those things are going down, focus, plug back into your passions, to your dreams, charge yourself back up. The power of hope is a real and renewable resource. Hope is always a guiding light even in your darkest days.

Hope and fear cannot occupy the same space, so invite the vibration of hope to stay. We hope for the best when someone is sick or in trouble but there's a deeper understanding to hope. Hope can be a life-supporting force that gives us more control over how each day unfolds. Most people don't realize hope has enormous power. Everyone knows that life is always uncertain.

The fear of uncertainty and trying to control every detail of your life is the path of fear and anxiety, which leads to a life of insecurity, low expectations, and unfulfilment. The other path is to embrace uncertainty for its creative potential and its ability to make life new every day. If you take this path, life becomes ever-expanding creative fulfillment and security, a strong sense of self and steady process of awakening moving forward in that hope becomes very different. Instead of being a form of wishful thinking it becomes an intention that the universe carries out the purpose to ignite your vision.

Hope and faith can be a real force in your life. Is there an aspect of your life you hope will get better: a job that has stopped being challenging, a crappy unfulfilling relationship or simply a problem to be solved? Have you been hoping things will get better as a whole? Your life journey begins today. The first step is to ask yourself how hope is working for you right now. Are you moving steadily in the direction of fulfilling your hopes and dreams? Begin to discover that hope and faith are your source of strength. They support life from the very centre of your being.

Hope is always available. When we see life through a lens of hope everything can change.

This can be a challenging practice when you're in the centre of the storm but what looks like a dark patch at the outset can actually be a beautiful turning point. It's hard to see when you're going through a shit storm but there's always a rainbow behind the clouds. You can choose to feel loved even when there's a conflict. You can make the choice to expand your awareness and make positive choices on the foundation of hope and faith. When we are faced with a difficult situation, we have the choice of two reactions: hope or despair. When you choose hope you open your mind and can then begin to imagine other possibilities when you're facing significant life-changing situations. Too many people lose hope after the smallest of resistance and will often put off a courageous life improving course of action. I say go for it now. Hope is in this moment and every moment. Don't waste another second.

Real hope is a quality that exists in consciousness like that for joy and love. When the situation is hopeless we're not seeing clearly to activate hope. It happens now because hope is a part of our present awareness, otherwise hope is a dream of the past or the future.

Everything depends on how we choose to relate to uncertainty but just like life's constant stream of challenges, hope and faith allows you to embrace uncertainty and remain optimistic. Through this inner strength of hope, we can work through a crisis in uncertain times. When self-doubt appears you feel weak and afraid not because of outside forces beyond your control but because of the self-doubt that comes from being disconnected from your true self. When you doubt yourself you can't trust anyone or anything. The most loving and trustworthy person will and can only reflect your inner selfs fear of being let down, which is the same as expecting to be let down. People who have been routed by failure such as finances and personal relationships typically believe circumstances outside themselves are at fault.

Trust and belief are two other qualities that support our journey of hope. If you look for an outcome but don't believe it will happen you're giving yourself false hope. If you have no trust that a good outcome is possible that truth defeats hope.

Trust and belief are two things we have control over. Everyone has core beliefs about how life works out. These core beliefs are about what we think is fair and unfair, right and wrong. When someone believes life is unfair they miss the point that they are responsible for creating their own reality equal to the vibration they set forth. This negates the victim mentality and promotes the realization that we are fully empowered to take the actions and make the choices and embrace a way of thinking and being that will bring us the happiness in life we desire. It's up to you and it's on you to create the reality you desire.

Gratitude is the ultimate spiritual solution to help you connect to the power of hope. With hope, you can experience a feeling and sense of peace overtake you that burns off doubt and anxiety. Through hope, faith, and trust you are lifted, connecting to yourself without judgment. This is an essential part of the journey of hope.

Most people focus attention only on the level of the problem rather than the level of the solution. Imagine your problem is trying to find a book in a dark cluttered basement, and you cannot see clearly, and you keep banging your head. If you focus on the problem, you try to protect your head and squint harder as you keep searching through every box. If you focus on the solution you pause, find the light switch and turn on the lights so you can see everything clearly and then find the book. Expanding our awareness through meditation is like turning on the lights. We automatically open ourselves to the universe of alternatives. That light of consciousness that gives us the ability to solve the problem knowing our expanded awareness always offers a solution, in every circumstance we may encounter.

Be open and alert and know that hope is always on your side. We can find a reason to hope in every situation. So many of us look to the future for a moment of happiness or contentment: "I will be happy when". We adopt this thinking because we are not present in the moment, allowing our true spiritual self to get in the flow of now, in the present where we can find a place of happiness.

To be one with life is being one with the present, to become self-aware. You don't live through your life but your life lives through you. You're not playing, you're being played. Life is the dancer, and you are the dance. We are the instrument that universal source energy flows through. All you need to do is let go of the paradigms holding you back and go and become immersed with the flow of universal source energy. Stop yourself from blocking your own potential, believe and trust and go with the natural flow. Understand in life we will always be learning but with practice, you will discover the quest for awareness and self-enlightenment much easier than most people believe.

When you open your heart you will find the power of hope.

By activating hoping awareness you bring new possibilities to light within yourself. You do not have to force yourself to see hope; you summon it as part of who you are. Learn to trust and let optimism arise naturally to activate hope. We bring attention to our presence of awareness. This awareness is like the stream on which our feelings and thoughts of sensations are projected.

Compassion flows with feeling. When you open your heart you will find the power of hope.

Compassion is another quality of our consciousness that gives hope its power. Compassion creates an intimate bond from heart to heart of being open and accepting in everyday life with someone who becomes a close ally, friend, or lover. At first, feelings can be uncertain and vulnerable. Compassion, however, is not distracted and is not restricted; it shines its light through and melts uncertainty and feelings of vulnerability.

BELIEF

One of our most overlooked superpowers in life is the unbelievable power of belief. Perhaps the greatest power of all is the power of belief. Develop and focus your desire, your passion, and belief for what you aspire to accomplish.

Believe in yourself, believe that you are deserving and worthy, believe that with persistence and a burning desire rooted deep within your heart that you simply cannot be denied your success.

From birth through our formative years we have been programmed to the Matrix, given our beliefs and habits of thought from our parents, our peers, our environment, and surroundings. To live, absorb and embrace a belief system that is for more the benefit of others than for us, that does not serve our best interests and in fact, is self-sabotaging our potential growth and success.

What do you really desire; what do truly want? You need to keep your ambitions in front of you to keep the flame of motivation going. Your belief needs to embrace a mindset of expectancy. Expectancy is a belief that not only is it possible for you but you can do it and have personal control. It's the autonomy that says I know what I believe in, my ability to figure this out, and I know I can move the needle of progress forward. You expect your dreams to happen and you expect that you have the strength and confidence to make them happen.

Beliefs can empower us or cage us in forever. Beliefs are
that powerful.

When you trust your true self you believe in the part of you that knows you can do this. You can do better. The key to trust is going within, following your intuition, and facing the unknown. You control what you believe. Your beliefs determine what you manifest in your life when you allow yourself to be vulnerable. You can trust that no matter what happens the universal source energy loves you, encourages you, walks beside you, and lives within you nurturing your greatest self and source of your greatest empowerment waiting for your expression. Now some may read that passage and think is he saying that God loves us, walks beside us, nurtures us and lives within us as our greatest source of empowerment and the answer is hell yes and my good old buddy, loving Jesus as well. But that is me and for people that are not religious or believe a different religion they are free to call God, the infinite intelligence, the superconscious mind or whatever they please.

It's no wonder so many people struggle. We are wandering around lost in a self-created prison based upon self-sabotaging inefficient belief systems we got from others who were just as lost, preconditioned and brainwashed as we are, and we are completely oblivious to the fact. Have you ever stopped and thought about why you value and buy in to certain habits and beliefs that you've simply been conditioned by people your culture and environment growing up to believe. Have you stopped to think whether some of these beliefs are limiting your potential and just why the hell you still believe them?

Imagine you're a vulnerable toddler, you can't fend for yourself you look up to see these adult humans much larger than you that feed, clothe, and protect you. They teach you the language, how to read, and little tricks that make your life easier. So if they tell you to cheer for the Vancouver Canucks and hate the Toronto Maple Leafs why wouldn't you and if they told you to believe that one political party is better than another why wouldn't you and if they told you to believe one race of people is superior to another why wouldn't you? So, if they were to tell you that you're too stupid, too fat, too short, too ugly, that you are not worthy, that you're a loser you will never amount to anything in life, it is possible that you will come to the realization years later reading these words that you have been spending your entire life unaware as to why you've never felt fulfilled, happy, or whole and like someone who is deserving of success and good things in life. We are all riddled with insecurities and to make positive life-altering changes to our habits, beliefs, and perspective, way of living means facing the anxiety and fear that accompanies significant change that so many experience. The term associated with the ingrained negative neural pathways through-out your mind causing harmful self-sabotaging thought processes is Schema Scripts. These are cognitive processes within your mind and the role they play in social interactions and how you view and live your life each day can be determined by them, for better or worse. As far as processing new ways and thoughts to process your schema scripts (current ingrained way of thinking), you are more likely to accept information and influences that fit comfortably with how you mentally process life/reality, even if they are negative or harmful. They are the comfortable evil we've been conditioned to throughout our lifetime.

IMAGINATION AND CREATIVE VISUALIZATION

"Imagination is everything. It is the preview of life's coming attractions."
—Albert Einstein

"Imagination is the ability to form a mental image of something that is not perceived through the five senses. It is the ability of the mind to build mental scenes, objects or events that do not exist, are not present, or have happened in the past".
—Remez Sasson, *The Power of Imagination*

Creative Visualization describes a simple technique for creating the results you want in life.

Your imagination is the most powerful, creative force in the universe. It can transcend space and time and in your thoughts transport you to anywhere you want to go and be anything you want to be. It can tap you into the infinite field of potential where all probability already exists. Your imagination is the magnetic force to attract the thing imagined from the place of infinite probability to physical reality. Most people are oblivious to this reality and as a result don't take the time and effort to understand the essential and powerful creative role that imagination plays in our lives.

Imagination is more important and powerful than knowledge. Why, you might ask? Knowledge is limited to what is currently known and understood, imagination and its infinite nature stretches far beyond knowledge. The imagination manifests in various degrees. Depending on an individual's frequency and rate of vibration some can have highly developed imagination and visualization skills and for others lower on the frequency scale their manifestation power is weaker.

Daily practice of visualization meditation will increase your skill for utilizing your imagination's powers and ability to combine all your senses. The first thing that comes to mind when you think of visualizing with imagination is mind pictures. But you can also train your mind to visualize experiencing all the five senses. You can imagine the experience of sound, taste, smell, physical sensations or feelings of emotions. Mental pictures of the things you desire in combination with imagined visualization of the feelings and emotions of the things you want will more securely put you in the zone of imagining the full experience of your desires. Focusing on every detail concerning your wants increases your vibration and magnetism of attraction.

Imagination plays a lead role in everyone's life. We are all using our imagination whether we are consciously or unconsciously aware that we are. The creative power of imagination is the main ingredient for visualization, positive thinking, and affirmations. Positive emotion and heartfelt loving desire for your creative visualization are key and you must avoid the dark side of your imagination's great powers. We don't want to attract into our lives unwanted people and circumstances.

Lack of understanding of the power of visualization manifestation is why many people suffer difficulties, failures, and unhappiness in their lives. Unfortunately for most people, our survival emotions rule the day based on anxiety, stress, and fear so their thinking and belief system is predominantly negative. People don't condition themselves to have expectations of success; they think the worst and believe the way of the world is against them. Good or bad, our emotional focus dictates our destiny's direction. You must understand how to combine your imagination with creative visualization correctly immersed in a high vibration frequency of positive thinking and emotion.

PERSISTENCE

> "Nothing in this world can take the place of persistence. Talent will not: nothing is more common than unsuccessful men with talent. Genius will not: unrewarded genius is almost a proverb. Education will not: the world is full of educated derelicts. Persistence and determination alone are omnipotent."
> —Calvin Coolidge

> "Never quit. Never surrender."
> —Commander Peter Quincy Taggart, *Galaxy Quest*

> "Never, never, never quit."
> —Sir Winston Churchill

Persistence: firm or obstinate continuance in a course of action in spite of difficulty or opposition. T here is the challenge and there is the line drawn in the sand. I say strap on a set of balls, and go for it people!

The reality about persistence is if you quit you're done. You can't accomplish your dreams and aspirations if you stop reaching for them. Absolutely never quit, unless of course your idea is a very useless and stupid idea that you've somehow talked yourself into believing. Stay positive in that you are strengthening your mastery of the law of belief;

negative in that your belief is for a stupid ass plan that may not have been thought through and could cost you a lot of money and misery. This being said following a stupid ass plan is not the end of the world nor is it a mistake, at least you took action. The mistake would be to stop trying. Don't be defeated because one course of action doesn't work out. Failure is merely postponed success. The fact is the higher you set your sights the more likely you are to fail repeatedly along the way. Which means an absolutely critical component of high achievement is dogged perseverance in the face of failure.

"When the going gets tough ... the tough get going."
Bluto, *Animal House*

Never let your persistence and passion turn into their evil twins stubbornness and ignorance. Be smart and plan your strategy well before you take action, and if it is not working it's not a failure – it is an attempt that helped you discover a better way to accomplish your goal. Don't be too stubborn and ignorant and keep flogging a dead horse. Know when it's time to switch up your plan if you're not getting results. Your persistence in any given endeavour is determined by the clarity of your purpose. Patience, perspiration, and persistence will win the day but persistent stupidity/ignorance will win you nothing.

It's not going to be all hearts and roses things are going to be challenging from time to time. it's a little easier if we set our expectations. Understand there is going to be some dark days that will be tough and challenge you emotionally physically and financially not everything is going to be smooth. Embrace the opportunity to get behind it and learn by the challenges that life has to offer.

The five P's to be successful: you need a Purpose, you need Passion, you need an intelligently conceived Plan, you need the assistance of the right People and you need most importantly to be Persistent. Persistence is a consistent insistence that you refuse to stop trying until you accomplish your goal; you refuse to stop and you will stand against every opposition. Persistence is the fire in your being that will carry you through ridicule and rejection and whatever nastiness threatens to impede your journey.

> The strength of character you build through the experience of achievement through pitfalls, roadblocks, and hardship is as much a gift to yourself as the achievement itself.

A well-developed mindset of persistence is our best way to counter and prevail over our nemesis procrastination. The people who go the extra mile when the road gets bumpy are the ones who reap the rewards. And far too many people are pussy ass little bitches that give up at the first sign of resistance, so the lesson there in is to pull your socks up in the face of adversity people and don't succumb to being a pussy ass whiney little bitch! We overcome resistance with unrelenting persistence. In modern times, we want it now, and we want it just how we want it; we live in the era of instant gratification. To have good things in your life that you passionately desire is worth some struggle, hardship, and potential grief to attain. The strength of character you build through the experience of achievement through pitfalls, road-blocks, and hardship is as much a gift to yourself as the achievement itself. You're going to hit roadblocks and setbacks, disappointments, seemingly real bad luck that will feel like defeat, but you must not be defeated. Hitting the wall shows you who you are. You've got to dig deep and push through with courage, faith, and belief in yourself and your quest. You will come out on the other side better and stronger.

You will encounter defeats, but you must not be defeated. In fact, it is necessary to encounter the defeats so you can know who you are, what you can arise from and how you can still come out of it. Perseverance is the ability to keep going after defeat. Don't define each stumble or failure along the way, as they are only there to make you stronger. Try to see the other qualities and lessons that come forth and shape who you are as you go. Sometimes feelings of defeat, failure, and anxiety will sneak up on you. When they do, try to feed your courage instead of fuelling your fear.

Don't be afraid. Jump in knowing the universal source energy is always there to assist and guide you. Even if it's for some stupid ass plan that is destined for failure, the infinite intelligence always has your back. But know because the infinite intelligence is infinitely intelligent it will let your stupid ass plan fail so you can then come to the awareness that you were a dumbass and need to develop a better plan. But enough about being a potential dumbass with stupid ass plans.

Let's say you've got a great plan that you are passionate about. Hang on to hope and patience. People often think time is this thing that works against us but in the area of persistence, time is your friend. Another good buddy of persistence is our wise friend patience.

Stay on track and never stop trying to be confident and passionate and you will reach the top of the mountain. Chances are, however, there will be a gestation time for your visualization to manifest in physical reality, which will require faith and patience on your part. If you want to discover the omnipotence of persistence you must be willing to have an obsession and be driven and consumed by your quest, to do whatever it takes, taking the time and patience, intelligent planning, and approach to shaping and adjusting your strategy as you go.

Someone who is a big shot is no more than a little shot that just kept on shooting. If you find you think you've reached the end of your rope, tie a knot and hang the fuck on! Ambition and imagination will take you down the rocky path to success. Persistence is the dune buggy to get you there.

Whatever it is that defines your definite purpose, your heroic journey, your destiny it will not be given to you, you have to go and get it. It's not going to be easy to make your mark in the world. If it were, everybody would be doing it. So in closing folks remember, when you're on your mission of achievement, it is always too soon to quit.

MASTERMIND

A mastermind group is a tightly knit and supportive group of like-minded people who share a common goal/interest in working together with a passion to achieve maximum results.

If you plan to make some big moves and accomplish big goals you simply cannot succeed without employing the mastermind principle. It's great to identify your goals and objectives but you've got to take action as thoughts and dreams alone won't get you there. Better than just the actions of yourself is the actions of many, all coordinated towards the same mutual objective. There is a powerful metamorphosis that takes place within a mastermind group. Not only do you get all the different perspectives and talent each individual in the group can offer but the magnetic pull to magically manifest what is needed from the universe is exponentially increased. You can say law of attraction instead of magic but the awesome power of a group aligned with and determined to reach a mutual goal is unstoppable and can produce seemingly magical results.

Napoleon Hill introduced the concept of the mastermind in his book *Think and Grow Rich*. He explained the mastermind as "the coordination of knowledge and effort of two or more people, who work toward a definite purpose, in the spirit of harmony." He then said. "No two minds ever come together without thereby creating a third, invisible force, which may be likened to a third (The mastermind)."

When you combine your power with others toward a common vision/goal your combined power potential is super turbocharged to a power stratosphere that can only be attained through the mastermind principle, which is far beyond your power potential as an individual. The mastermind principle is all about leverage and power.

The vibrational potential of your subconscious mind by itself is immensely powerful. If you truly want a lift off to accelerate towards what you want and to make big moves and do big things it is necessary to command the earth-shattering vibrational potential of many human brains melding together in harmony towards a common goal

The personal benefits for mastermind group members are far reaching in that each member supports and feeds inspiration off one another in the form of a collective think tank. This is why it's important to select skilled people with a broad and diverse range of expertise. The collective thought processes of the group merge, which often leads to igniting timely and invaluable ideas. By sharing ideas and brainstorming strategies, struggles, roadblocks, thoughts, and feelings in general you remain open and receptive to various insights and ideas from other group members' varying perspectives. Being part of a smooth running effective mastermind group is win-win. You can advance your personal as well as your business aspirations while at the same time you contribute and provide the same valuable contribution and benefit to others. You've got their back and they have yours. The power of the mastermind serves two crucial and productive purposes: you get the collective benefit of fresh perspectives, strategies, and insights, but also provide the support, positive input, and reinforcement needed to keep focused on the desired outcome.

The benefits of being in an effective mastermind group stack up and become evident quickly. It offers both professional and emotional support and promotes an environment of efficiency, clarity, and focus. When joining or forming a mastermind group, there are a number of things that you will want to consider in advance: group size, scheduled meeting times, how often and how long, what is your mission statement, what is the group's ultimate collective vision, what is the direction and what is the expectation of accomplishment.

Mastermind meetings don't have to be overthought, over planned, or overcomplicated. A simple agenda that all the members can easily partake in and contribute to usually works best. If you truly want to get big things done and kick some major ass, you need to embrace and implement the united human power found within the mastermind group.

I will also mention that two human minds working in harmony with a collective vision is better than just one, and it cannot be understated that behind every successful man or woman throughout history you will consistently find a strong and loving partner with heartfelt commitment to supporting their heroic mission that ultimately becomes their combined heroic mission though only one of them might be more in the limelight.

CHAPTER 9
THE CONSCIOUS AND SUBCONSCIOUS MIND: APPLYING THE LAW OF ATTRACTION

"If you think in negative terms you will get negative results. If you think in positive terms you will get positive results."
—Norman Vincent Peale

We all have just one brain, one mind. There is a duality function within our minds that involves the conscious, objective, voluntary, waking mind and the subconscious, subjective, involuntary, sleeping mind. The conscious mind is your identity. It's the seed of your spirituality, your creative thinking, reasoning mind, and the subconscious mind is a stimulus-response mind. Like a recording database, it is habitual. It replays the programs that make up who you are and, unfortunately for most, the programs are comprised of other people's beliefs and habits and are limiting and self-sabotaging and not serving your wishes and desires. The subconscious mind drives our behaviours and beliefs. Things that at first get done through the function of the conscious mind, after much repetition the subconscious mind takes over as those things become second nature. Many of your actions throughout the course of an average day are programmed responses of your subconscious mind without you even being aware.

The relationship and interaction between your conscious and subconscious mind is where the key to mastering the law of attraction to your advantage lies. You can access your subconscious mind by practicing meditation.

What is the conscious mind?

The conscious mind controls everything that you do. It is responsible for reasoning and logical thought. Any voluntary action like scratching your bum, jumping over a puddle, any action you're aware that you're doing is the work of your conscious mind.

What is the subconscious mind?

The subconscious mind deals with all involuntary actions. Your bodily functions such as your heartbeat, breathing, and your body temperature is controlled by your subconscious mind. Your subconscious mind is also a supercomputer library, which records every memory and experience you've ever had. It drives your behaviours and beliefs. It is believed that your subconscious mind is tens of thousands more times powerful than the conscious mind.

Many of us are aware we have something called a subconscious mind but for most, that's where it ends. As previously mentioned, your subconscious mind is immensely powerful and when mastered and given the right instructions can manifest thoughts of potential reality into physical reality. It literally has the power to move mountains.

So let's look at unleashing and manifesting the awesome unequaled power of the subconscious mind. Manifestation is a fairly simple process and your subconscious mind is on the job busily manifesting at all times whether you are on board as an active participant or not.

You have a thinking mind and whatever you think, you can become. Whatever you can conceive within your mind you can achieve. You're going to draw into your life exactly what your thoughts are focused on most, whether it be good stuff or bad stuff, it's as simple as that. It is very important to be aware and believe in the immense power within your subconscious mind and that it is always at the ready to engage whatever marching orders you give it. It is for this reason what we think about, we become. Whatever it is that you really, really, really want you will get and whatever you really, really, really don't want you will also get because that is what you are intently focused on and as previously mentioned your subconscious mind does not distinguish between imagined or real, good or bad. It takes everything presented and runs with it to bring about manifestation. It is for this reason that you don't want to focus on the things in life that you are lacking because you will attract more lack of those things. For all the bad things and bad breaks that happen to you and the lack of things you wish you had you must man or woman up and accept that you alone are 100 per cent responsible for everything that happens to you in your life both good and bad with nobody and nothing else to pass the blame to.

The good news is that you're in control and once you become aware and get in the game and become actively involved, you can then shape and manifest the destiny you seek.

Think of your conscious mind as the captain of the ship sitting in the wheelhouse steering the ship, setting and charting the course for your destination. And think of your subconscious mind as the huge powerful ship with huge engines and propellers at the ready to take you wherever you want to go.

Unfortunately for many, they are snoozing and smoking pot in the wheelhouse, and the ship is drifting aimlessly in circles. Sometimes because people don't care enough to become actively involved, but often it's because people don't fully understand or believe the fact that the human mind is a very powerful transmitter/receiver capable of tapping into the infinite intelligence/superconscious mind, accessible to infinite wisdom, healing, and power. It lies within every one of us waiting for us at our beck and call, to give it development and expression.

You don't have to acquire this power. It comes stock with every human body and brain at birth. It resides within your subconscious mind, and you simply need to learn how, through meditation and daily practice in visualization and mind power exercises to activate and use it. Once you unleash this source of unlimited power and wisdom it will link with the infinite intelligence/superconscious mind that exists in every living thing, the invisible ether that surrounds the earth and the air we breathe. It is the power that moves the earth, guides the planets in their course and causes the sun to shine.

> We have not nearly tapped the potential of the human brain. It is more powerful than the most powerful supercomputer.

We have not nearly tapped the potential of the human brain. It is more powerful than the most powerful supercomputer. You have 100 billion neurons that make up the brain. The brain can work in a multitude of different sequences, patterns, and combinations. With new discoveries in neural science and quantum physics, we are just beginning step outside the box and discover what is possible.

> There is a huge gap between what we know and what we do.

Your mind is packed with information, but, there is a huge gap between what we know and what we do. We have phenomenal intellectual factors. The conscious mind has the ability to accept or reject a problem. With fear, we are led to accept the things we don't want and reject the things we do want. Almost everybody does it as we are all slave to the Matrix consistently there in place to restrict and repress our greater aspirations. This is because the negative paradigms and negative neural pathways established in our mind don't want us to dare to dream and dare to do. For some, gaining a better understanding of you is not that easy, as discussed in chapter 1. It can be scary tapping into parts of our personality with which we are not that familiar.

The subconscious mind will and must accept anything you give to it and cannot reject it. The key is that the subconscious mind cannot differentiate between what you imagine and what is real. If you can visualize yourself doing something, you have the talent inside to do it.

So why, the question might be asked, don't we do it?

In our first years, our subconscious mind was filled with whatever was going on around us. This is where the image of you was formed.

It's this self-image that really keeps us locked into where we are. It is this concept of our self-image that will cause us to go where we want to go. Self-image is just part of the paradigm. It is the same as culture and environment. It is nothing but group habit. A paradigm is a multitude of habits. This is the way we are programmed and woven into the inner fabric of the Matrix. The food we like, the language we speak, our whole and entire perception of reality is controlled in this area and was locked in at a very early age. It is not taught in school how to reprogram our minds and alter negative paradigms. In our conscious mind, each and every one of us has the power to reject the bad stuff and only feed our subconscious mind creative good stuff. But unfortunately for most, we do not, so many people are not entirely aware or believe these paradigms even exist.

There are people out there with a wealth of superior knowledge but often their results are less than impressive. That's because results are and always will be determined by the paradigms. To change your results, you must alter your paradigms and rewire your subconscious mind with new positive neural pathways. Paradigms based on fear are what hold people back, forcing them to stay where they are. The conscious mind is the gatekeeper to what thoughts and ideas and instructions are sent to our subconscious mind and the conscious mind will only send information that is in harmony with the established paradigms. The paradigm controls the vibration of your mind and body.

The body is a molecular instrument. It's a mass of molecules at a very high speed of vibration. The vibration that the body is in at a conscious level, we call feeling. When you say you feel this way or that, you are in fact describing the state of vibration you are in. We choose thoughts in harmony with the vibration we are in because it's what we know and is comfortable to us. The problem is that we become slaves to this precondition. We are in a prison, but, there are no bars on the doors; we can walk out any time we want.

We live in a prison of paradigms cultivated and impressed in our minds throughout our years of living, that restrict, repress, and suffocate our power of imagination and thought vibration to manifest great things in our life. The irony is that the prison gates are wide open and we can walk out any time, but we've been programmed to embrace the cozy, familiar, predictability of it all. We've become good buddies with the prison guards and like Ricky from the show *Trailer Park Boys* where he spends Christmas in jail with all the weed, free meals, and booze he needs, we feel it's a pretty safe cool place to be though we are in fact incarcerated.

At the circus, they chain the adult elephants with what looks like a relatively small chain around their ankle and this chain around the ankle goes into a stake in the ground. The elephant could easily rip that stake out of the ground with its size and strength but any time they feel the slightest pressure on the chain they instantly stop. The reason being is that when they are very small they put an identical chain around their ankle, and the chain is not put to a stake in the ground. It is bolted to cement, so no matter how much effort the baby elephant puts into trying to escape they cannot escape. Day after day, the baby elephants will struggle and pull and pull until finally one day they give up, and they realize that there is no way no matter how hard they struggle that they can escape. At that point the elephant is trained that all you have to do is tap a stake in the ground because the moment the elephant moves his leg and feels the tightening of the chain he instantly quits. We are all adult elephants chained to self-imposed limitations by negative, self-sabotaging, limiting paradigms, and negative neural pathways established in our subconscious mind, from which we could easily break free.

I read the elephant story years ago and the message is clear, but takes a minute to let it sink in how much we put limits on what we think we can accomplish, be and desire because we've been brainwashed and programmed since childhood to think that way. The deeply ingrained limiting paradigms represent the stake hammered in the ground the adult elephant could easily rip out. The prison gates are wide open, and a limitless road of opportunities await, but we are hypnotized and programmed to stay in the box. Right now, right this moment is a perfect time to say, "Fuck that shit, I won't be ruled over by these negative paradigms/schema scripts any further. I'm on a mission to identify them, break them down and rewire my whole perception of what is possible and that there is truly nothing holding me back other than my restricted beliefs, habits, and thinking."

Do you want to live a normal mundane life or do you want to live an exciting extraordinary life? I like how Bob Proctor said of how "so many people tiptoe through life hoping to make it safely to death."

People are scared to risk anything or take a chance because they fear criticism if they try and fail. Their fear of failing and those that might ridicule them stop them more than their desire to achieve pushed them forward. Be prepared for when you try to step out from the herd and live a more inspired productive life reaching higher with your goal setting and aspirations for self-growth. People around you will say, "Hey man, what are you doing? None of that stuff could or will possibly happen for you. Forget about your pipe dreams. Come back to reality and get back in line with the rest of us sheep and live a nice quiet uninspired predictable and safe life of conformity." It's amazing how many great ideas and plans have been abandoned because of a few people shooting it down and talking negatively.

Everyone is susceptible and insecure. Until you reprogram yourself to intuitively know the naysayers are full of shit and have no vision of their own, you won't see that they are invested in you staying in the comfortable little box right alongside them. You control your destiny. Do not listen to any of these negative nellies, be they friends, family or whoever.

You are the architect of your own destiny.

Accept that we create everything that happens in our lives both good and bad and that we alone are ultimately 100 per cent responsible for what happens. Realize that life does not simply happen to us as we roll with the punches. We have the power to shape, mold and manifest whatever it is we want in life. You are the architect of your own destiny.

So, how do we break free? When does the conscious mind dare to consider a radical idea like taking a risk, going on that vacation, moving to that new town, buying that new car you saved for? As long as this idea resides only in the conscious mind, without being passed forward to the subconscious mind, it remains an intellectual exercise never to come to fruition.

Your central nervous system is the most complex electrical system in the universe. The moment you take the idea from your intellect and impress it upon your subjective mind is when magical shit hits the fan, so to speak :). Like Tom Hanks, in the movie *Outcast,* trying to get past the big wave in his little homemade raft. Your radical, cool unconventional idea is introduced to the subconscious mind. The body moves into defensive vibration. On a conscious level we begin to experience doubt. Doubt turns into an emotion called fear. And fear is expressed through the body as anxiety. Just as the person starts to get emotionally involved to move ahead, they hit the paradigm wall of negative neural pathways riddled throughout our subconscious mind chaining us to the Matrix of mediocrity. The wave comes crashing down, smashing your little makeshift raft of ambition and dreams to tiny bits. Sending you hurtling back to the beach where it's cozy and safe. You cancel the sale or trip. You stay in the job you don't like. It's not ideal but, it's our comfort zone.

Get energized. Break the trend. Get emotionally involved and embrace a radical, daring new way of thinking, and expel those feelings of fear, doubt, and anxiety and smash through that psychological wall like Bruce Lee on nitro; release yourself and break free of the Matrix of conformity and mediocrity.

Learn to control what's going on in your inside, plus you want to block all the negative crap from the outside. If you're worried about lack that you're not going to get what you need, you won't look after what you need to look after. This feeling transmutes and is changed into an emotional state of fear. So many people live and are dictated by fear. That fear is then expressed through the physical body and central nervous system and the body moves into a state of anxiety. Anxiety attracts disease and decay. Do not let fear make you its little bitch of conformity.

Many people think their lives are unfulfilling because of their circumstances; the fact is you ultimately control your circumstances. You need to create the circumstances that are aligned in favour of what you want in life and the lifestyle you want to live.

Every day is an opportunity to increase your knowledge. Through daily study and practice, you develop an understanding of the principles of mind power, auto-suggestion, and visualization, the power of creativity, imagination, persistence, faith, and belief.

You want to get unplugged from the Matrix, tap into the transmitting power of your subconscious mind and get tuned in to vibrational harmony between what it is you want and desire to manifest within the quantum field. This is the goal.

As our incredibly powerful subconscious mind reacts and feels so does our body. That's because the subconscious mind and our body are one and the same. Think of your entire body from your lower extremities to your heart and upper body as representing your subconscious mind. Our mind and body have primal tendencies and reactions genetically imprinted through centuries of human evolution. Our fight or flight response from back in the caveman days when we had to hightail to avoid the sabre-toothed tiger making us into a meal is one of them. In the wild, when a gazelle gets chased by a predator it takes flight with high adrenaline then after the chase calms down and goes back to grazing like nothing happened.

For humans, our survival emotions are derived from the hormones of stress same as the gazelle. Unfortunately, we have a tendency to internalize these negative emotions as opposed to releasing them. What is even worse is we have tendencies to become subconsciously addicted to negative emotions such as stress, anger, fear, sadness, resentment, and frustration. These emotions all trip the brain with a rush of energy that we subconsciously become addicted to. Sadly there are people addicted to their own frustration, suffering, and guilt.

Seventy per cent or more of the time, most people are living by the hormones of stress whether you know it or not. Very few people are living in the present moment. If you're not in the present moment then you are running some sort of program, you are for all effective reasons plugged into the Matrix. If you're not present, your body's already programmed to be in the future or in the past.

People find themselves living on Matrix auto pilot, replicating all the same habits and behaviours they've done for the last 20 or 30 years, locked into a linear timeline where their future and their past seem to be exactly the same like Bill Murray in the movie "Ground Hog Day". We live in two states of mind: we either live in a state of survival or we live in a state of creation.

The state of survival is seated in bad stuff, stress emotions and the state of creation is seated in good stuff, the emotions of joy and love. Regrettably, the majority of people on the planet for the most part of their breathing moments live by the primal survival state of stress and anxiety. Every time you have a reaction to stress something in your life that you consider, threatening or that you are uncertain about, remember these emotions of stress are the exact emotions of anger, hatred, judgement, fear, anxiety, pain and suffering, hopelessness, and powerlessness. The majority of people spend the majority of their living breathing waking moments reciprocating those emotional states and those emotional states endorse the ego to be selfish, self-indulgent, self-centered, and self-important. Those chemicals of stress long-term begin to break the body down thinking about our problems or some future worst case scenario. The brain begins to signal the unconscious mind/body when we begin to feel those emotions that are connected to past experiences. It then believes it's in the past experience so you condition the body to either live in the past or live in the future as opposed to being present in the moment.

The number one ingredient when you're lost and engaged in doing something really cool is that you are in the present. When we are living and reacting in survival mode as most people do most of the time all of the survival emotions, hormonal centers, and adrenal glands are all centered in the lower part of the body.

We need to embrace a state of creation and emotions of love and joy, these energies will then become centred in the upper body in your heart chakra. As your emotional state moves to your heart you become less analytical and less judgemental. When you're in a state of love, joy and inspiration, that creative state of being is when the body/

subconscious mind is liberated from the chains of those very strong negative emotions.

Your body, your central nervous system, and your subjective unconscious, subconscious minds are one and the same, which together as one represent one of the most powerful forces in the universe that for the majority of people remains an untapped resource. The truth is, most people live their entire lives oblivious to and hardly scratch the surface of manipulating this colossal power source to their advantage.

Many people have no clue of the infinite power potential of the subconscious mind. Many people also have no clue of the power of the human heart, which centers the creative loving, joyful state of consciousness.

Embrace the positive, love energy, creative, magical power of feeling, thinking and aspiring with your heart. While our brain has an electrical and magnetic field, they are both comparatively weak to the human heart. The heart is about 100,000 times stronger electrically and up to 5,000 times stronger magnetically than the brain. This is important because the physical world as we know it is made of those two fields: electrical and magnetic fields of energy.

> "Physics tells us that if we can change either the magnetic field or the electrical field of the atom, we literally change that atom and its elements within our body and this world. The human heart is designed for both."
> —Gregg Braden, HeartMath Institute

The upside of the movie *The Secret* is that it brought awareness of the law of attraction and mindpower to millions of people. The downside is that many of those people came to the thinking that whatever we think about and want we can have. This analogy is certainly true but as far as empowering the law of attraction there is much much more to it than that.

To start with, the law of attraction is a secondary law; the law of vibration is a primary law. We can only attract those things that match up with our level of vibrational frequency be it high or low. If we want to listen to an FM station but we are tuned into an AM frequency, it's simply never going to happen. Simply thinking a thought and having a wish is not enough to bring it to manifestation. Here is a tip that many people who attempt to empower the law of attraction are not aware of, and it's why so many fail.

To empower the law of attraction you have to harness and channel the electrical, magnetic energy of your human heart to raise your vibration to its highest frequency; to the level that you can tap into the universal source energy and link your subconscious mind/body/self to the infinite intelligence to manifest your desires and aspirations. Read this last excerpt a couple times more to digest and internalize and fully understand it, because it's that important. The physical immense power of your heart is your key ally. Many think that love feeling and heart feeling is a metaphoric vision created within our mind and that our physical hearts only job is to just pump the blood. Not the case mofo! Your heart is mega powerful and the catalyst for all your ambitions hopes and dreams.

Love energy is the most positive and powerful energy in existence and this energy is centered in the human heart. Love energy does not emote from your brain, it channels from your heart and transmits its vibrational energy through your entire body, which is one and the same with the subconscious mind.

You must decide and define quite intentionally what it is you want and then develop a burning, focussed, and quite literally heartfelt desire, combined with faith, belief, and persistence to the attainment and manifestation of your goal.

To become pure consciousness, to become self-aware in a high state of positive vibration, to become truly enlightened and in a state of creation you become nobody, nothing. You move into the element of time and space where you feel connected to something greater, correlated to the infinite intelligence and universal source of pure love energy

When we're in the primal survival state we feel only concerned about the self. Whereas in the creative state we are in a selfless state no longer connected to the ego. The ego is out-of-the-way and that is called the natural state of being in pure consciousness. To make this change we have to step away from the known and embrace and step into the unknown. Our programmed Matrix consciousness is trained to think that we're moving into a place that's highly threatening. If you understand that you have a part in your creation of the unknown then it becomes an adventure, something exciting and not so threatening.

CHAPTER 10
THE SCIENCE OF MIND POWER

The Human Brain is at the centre of the quest to release yourself from the Matrix as this invisible Matrix prison in which people are conditioned to reside exists within our brains.

In this chapter, we explore recent scientific discoveries of brain function and some scientific terms explaining how our miraculous brains work. Let's start by taking a quick look at the brain, its many cool parts, and how they function.

THE MEDULLA OBLONGATA

The medulla arguably performs the most important function of the brain. Its functions are to keep you alive as it deals with the involuntary subconscious autopilot tasks that don't involve conscious thought. It controls and regulates the operations of breathing, digestion, and keeping your heart beating. As a part of the brain stem, it helps convey neural info from the brain to the spinal cord.

THE CEREBELLUM

The cerebellum is extremely important in that it is in charge of everyday voluntary functions given their marching orders from the conscious, active mind such as walking, talking, balance and all purposeful motor functions and muscle coordination.

THE HYPOTHALAMUS

The hypothalamus is responsible for motivational behaviour such as hunger and thirst and regulates our body temperature.

THE AMYGDALA

The amygdala is the center for motivation and emotional behaviour. It is responsible for the response of memory of emotions, especially fear.

THE HIPPOCAMPUS

The hippocampus is involved in the storage of long-term memory, and emotional responses, which includes all past knowledge and experiences.

THE THALAMUS

The thalamus helps regulate a person's sleep and wake cycles. It registers and receives information being relayed to the brain related to vision, hearing, taste, and other bodily sensations, and it sends these signals on to the cerebral cortex. The Thalamus in many ways serves as a relay center to the brain.

THE PONS

Besides the medulla oblongata, your brainstem also has a structure called the pons.

The pons serves as a message station between several areas of the brain, especially the cerebrum and the cerebellum. The pons also plays a key role in breathing, sleeping and dreaming.

THE BRAIN

Ok, now let's look at the left and right hemispheres of the brain. For people who wonder why in politics the left-wing parties are considered liberal hippie, help single mothers, and protect the planet and why right-wing parties are considered to be pro-corporate big business and special interests groups, we need to look no farther than the functions of the left and right hemispheres of the brain. The two hemispheres can be compared to steering a sailboat in that if you want the boat to go right you have to push left on the rudder and if you want to go left you must push right on the rudder. It can be confusing believe me as I incurred some harsh comments and fists in the air when I almost steered my friend's sailboat into another sailing out of Granville Island one nice sunny day when they let me captain the boat for a brief stint. After the incident I was quickly relieved of my duties as a beer was put in my hands in place of the rudder, which was fine with me at the time.

The Right Hemisphere

The right brain hemisphere is in control of the left side of your body and is the more imaginative, creative side of the brain. It is nonverbal and intuitive, using pictures, visualizations rather than words, insight, and philosophical thinking. These are all attributes of the right hemisphere of the brain, pulling from the more creative and artistic areas of thought.

The Left Hemisphere

The left brain hemisphere is in control of the right side of your body and is the more analytical and problem-solving side of the brain responsible for language along with mathematical thinking.

Corpus Callous

The corpus callosum is a good friend to the left and right brain hemispheres as it is responsible for transmitting neural messages between them, allowing for communication between the two hemispheres.

Cerebral Cortex

I've saved the best for last. The cerebral cortex serves as the seat of our conscious reasoning mind responsible for higher thought processes. This developed part of the human brain is what sets us apart from all other mammals. The cortex is divided into four lobes: the frontal lobe, parietal lobe, occipital lobe, and temporal lobe. Each oversees the processing of different categories of sensory information, from visual processing, movement, speech, emotions, etc.

The conscious reasoning mind imprints upon the subconscious mind, it takes it as its marching orders to manifest it to physical reality. Once again I bring your attention to the fact the subconscious mind cannot distinguish the difference between what is real or imagined and does not care if the tasks are for good or bad and it never takes time off. It is constantly manifesting our current reality whether we are actively aware and involved with the process or not. As Ernest Nightingale said you can plant the seed of nightshade deadly poison or you can plant corn seeds and that's what will grow. Immensely powerful, every vision you've ever seen awake or dreaming your subconscious mind has recorded. It is a source of wisdom, intelligence, and healing power beyond your wildest dreams.

Up until the last 30 years or so, not much was known about the human brain. Your brain contains 100 billion nerve cells, give or take, forming trillions of connections. These connections are called synapses. These synaptic connections are formed when neurons form new dendrites and axons, the threadlike extensions that connect one brain cell to another. Neurons are specialized cells found within the nervous system. Their function is to relay information to muscle, gland, and nerve cells. This communication contact point is referred to as Synapses.

Our brains are not hard-wired as previously believed. However, it is fact that your brain can be rewired. And this is a good thing. The old scientific belief was that the adult brain was hard-wired and after critical developmental periods in childhood, our brains were set and could change no further. As science has now proved, this belief is farthest from the truth. Yes, when we were young our brains were more like a sponge absorbing information in the theta state and yes that's when many false and harmful paradigms first made their home in your brain.

Our brains are also imprinted over centuries of years with each evolving generation creating what is your present-day genetic memory.

But the truth and the good news recently scientifically proven is that the adult brain has the ability to reorganize itself, both physically and functionally, forming new neural connections throughout life. This miraculous ability is called neural plasticity.

The are no connecting wires in our brains but there is circuitry throughout the living tissue.

This circuitry is shaped and molded by our thoughts, memories, emotions, and experiences.

More importantly, they are also reshaped by thoughts, desires, memories, and experiences.

The more neuroscientists discover about the brain the more they discover hidden powers.

Our brain does not only interpret the world, it creates it. Whatever you can visualize, imagine, or desire can be yours if you understand the process of how to properly channel your mind and actions.

This is the most important message of this book, *The Secret, Think and Grow Rich,* and others. Throughout our lifetime, it is possible for your brain to evolve, rewire and improve to be more empowered. The gift is there for everyone. This potential is stock issue with every brain God hands out. However your brain, unfortunately, cannot do what it thinks it cannot do. Here again, I'm talking about the conditioned schema scripts in our thinking and daily habits, the limits we needlessly restrain ourselves to.

Let's talk about glycine and glutamate.

GLYCINE:
Glycine is an amino acid, a building block for protein. It is the simplest possible amino acid. It is not a well-known term but our body is strengthened by the use of Glycine every day and allows it to work properly.

Glycine is the second most widespread amino acid found in human enzymes and proteins, which is why it has roles in nearly every part of the body. It is the major inhibitory neurotransmitter, it modulates excitatory neurotransmission (brings to action) a subtype receptor of glutamate. This receptor name is N-methyl-D-aspartate (NMDA).

GLUTAMATE:
Glutamate is a most powerful and abundant excitatory neurotransmitter in the nervous system. It accounts for the majority of synaptic connections in the brain.

Let's talk about the intellectual phase of the brain where the old ingrained paradigms/schema scripts and negative neural pathways deal with the introduction of new responses, new ways of thinking, new actions, and belief systems. As soon as you ask yourself why do I think this way, or that why do I love this thing and why do I hate that other thing, we enter into the element of intellect. Intellect is the way in which your brain has evolved the balance of both what we fear is not possible for us and what we desire/wish could be possible for us. Excitatory neurotransmitters like glutamate help strategize for what we desire and inhibitory neurotransmitters like glycine help counterbalance to keep our emotions in check. Our intellect and emotions do the constant synaptic dance of yin and yang between the two inhibitory and excitatory neurotransmitters. There is a struggle and neurological drama that subtly rages on within your brain. The ongoing ever spinning carousel ride of interaction between intellect and emotion creates a state of internal discourse that resonates throughout your brain through every waking hour. The decision to be made is between favouring the more hard-wired reaction response or new unknown responses.

This explains in scientific terms the struggle I keep mentioning between how our minds have been conditioned and programmed to the Matrix and how our creative imaginative mind wants to introduce new ways of thinking and being but must meet up with the badass paradigms reverberating the negative self-sabotaging schema scripts engrained in our psychology. These are the gatekeepers of the subconscious mind and must be overcome to initiate real and empowering changes to our habits and overall way of living/thinking.

Let's look at "fight or flight" vs "rest and digest"

We've all heard the term "fight or flight" referring to our primal caveman days response of the nervous system, the sabre-tooth tiger is chasing and wants to eat us and our body reacts to the stress of the situation. Not so well known is the equally cool term "rest and digest" response. This system is locked into the more relaxed and chill functions of the body. When we are more centered and in harmony, connected to source energy we are relaxed and chill. This state helps maintain long-term good health. These two systems exist within a larger system named the autonomic nervous system, which manages the function of our eternal organs.

Most people, unfortunately, hover in a stress influenced state of consciousness and can develop adrenal fatigue, where the fight or flight response is being activated too often, prompting our body's adrenal glands to respond, releasing large amounts of stress hormone like cortisol. Chronically elevated stress levels can long-term deplete your internal organs of materials they need to construct new neurotransmitters and hormones.

The part of the autonomic nervous system responsible for "fight or flight" response is called the sympathetic nervous system which prepares for the physical challenge (fight) or prepares for retreat (flight).

The part of the autonomic nervous system responsible for "rest and digest" response is called the parasympathetic system, which helps produce a state of balance in the body.

In these modern times in the Western world, most people find themselves experiencing some level of chronic stress in their daily lives.

The action of empowering your parasympathetic nervous system, in effect, reduces the impact of your sympathetic nervous system, which in turn reduces the stress on your immune and digestive system as well as your heart and more.

Let's look at the vagus nerve

The vagus nerve is the longest and largest cranial nerve in the body, beginning at the base of the skull and extending throughout the body, regulating all major bodily functions.

The vagus nerve interfaces with the parasympathetic nervous system, to control your heart, lungs, and core area. This action can dissipate the body's cortisol levels and reduce stress as your body chills and relaxes.

Here again is where the awesome power of meditation can be used to induce a state of calmness and relaxation to stimulate your vagus nerve and activate your parasympathetic nervous system. Mindfulness meditation is effective as well as meditations incorporating RB resistance breathing or chanting e.g."Ohm" or "Aum" the practice of yoga is also a popular way to stimulate the vagus nerve. Even activities that you enjoy like a good chess game or a nice relaxing spa day with a massage or healthy exercise activities like running, skiing, swimming, biking, roller blading, etc. help activate the rest and digest response, which is where we want to be as much as humanly possible.

As Bobby McFerrin says, "Don't worry be happy."

Now let's look at Epigenetics

Epigenetics is the study of modification of gene expression, which is not caused by changes in the genetic DNA code itself. The old thinking of the scientific community was that genes were the end all and be all of what our personal genetic blueprint was to be with no modifications or alterations. Recent studies contradict the old school theory. Epigenetics is a fairly young science, we've known about the epigenome since the early '70s but only in the last 20 years have scientists discovered the effect these epigenetic tags have on the human genome and that this effect can, in turn, be passed on to future generations

'Who you are is written in both pen and pencil. Things written in pen you can't change. That's DNA. But things written in pencil you can. We cannot control 30% of our genetic makeup, however that means we can control 70% with things like: lifestyle, diet, exercise, what we put on our skin, stress, etc." The epigenome sits on top of the genome; the epigenome is what tells your genes to switch on or off, like a light switch.

Epigenetics means "above genetics".

The epigenome cannot change your DNA, but it can control which genes within different cells in your body are expressed. As gene controller, Epigenetics is about the changes initiated throughout the course of your life and the genetic legacy to be passed down to your kids and grandkids. Life experiences can cause genes to awaken, become active, switch on and to also put to sleep, become dormant, switch off. Every action throughout your daily life influences chemical modifications within your genes some – switched on some switched off.

Throughout your body there are literally billions of cells each containing your DNA. Instructions are given to the cells from tiny hydrogen compounds called methyl groups.

The methyl groups attach to a gene and can switch that gene off to non-expression or switched on to be active. In addition, there exist histones. Histones are proteins that the DNA spools and winds itself around. Histones control how loosely or tightly wound the DNA will be. If tight, the expression of that gene is repressed and if loose the expression of that gene is enhanced. The methyl groups work and manipulate as an on-off switch whereas the histones are more like a volume knob raising and lowering gene expression. They are like the software that gives instruction to genes whereas the human genome – your encoded DNA – can be compared to the hard drive. The genome does all the heavy lifting but the epigenome gives it its marching orders. The hardware stays the same throughout your life but the software can be changed and modified throughout your life. Why is this good news? You can change your lifestyle and state of mind to have a huge impact on changing your epigenetic code to a more positive, healthier empowering state.

Through mind power and alignment of the body and mind you are not confined to your genetics. We have the power to alter and rewire our epigenetic code. Rise up to the genetic call to arms, go deep within to evolve who you are, how you act and think, to break free from the Matrix, i.e. expand your enlightenment/self-awareness. Turbocharge for high personal vibrational energy for both attracting and projecting to and from the universe.

Let's take a look at the different brain wave vibration and frequencies of the human mind.

There are five states of consciousness for the human brain. In order of highest to the lowest frequency they are Gamma, Beta, Alpha, Theta, and Delta.

Gamma: is the highest frequency and this is when your conscious mind is doing most of the work for intricate learning and high processing of information.

Beta: this is also the frequency used primarily by the conscious mind, while we are awake for logical/critical thinking, writing, reading, and socialization. In beta, we are perking up our neocortex and trying to create meaning between our outer world and the inner world. This is the mechanism of the brain to create coherence between what is going on outside of us and what is going on inside of us when we are functioning. In reality, you are creating beta wave patterns. Most people live and are most affected and influenced by their outer world taking life as it comes at them. The challenge is to go deep within your inner world where the key to change lies and manifest your outer world as you envision it to be.

Alpha: this is the frequency that connects our conscious and subconscious mind. Alpha's frequency range aligns between beta and theta and promotes feelings of deep relaxation. When you close your eyes and begin to illuminate the external environment you begin to reduce the amount of sensory information that is coming into your brain. Your brainwave patterns begin to slow down to the alpha brain waves. In alpha, the inner world tends to be more real than the outer world.

Theta: this is the frequency when the conscious mind gets out of the way and the subconscious mind takes over in a deeply relaxed semiotic (meaning-making) state. It is during this state of consciousness and to some degree alpha state as well, that the subconscious mind can be reprogrammed by means of meditation and listening to subliminal recordings while falling asleep. The great benefit of this technique is you can reprogram your subconscious mind with very little effort.

Delta: this represents the deepest state of sleep and relaxation. Delta waves are the slowest recorded waves in the human brain. In this state of deep sleep, your body can repair and do maintenance of tissue, bone, and muscle, and add strength to your immune system.

So how is it exactly that you may very well be living the grand sum of others' beliefs and habits, hypnotized, spinning around blindly in the Matrix on mental autopilot?

Our brain's ability to transition through various states of consciousness has a huge influence on how effectively we manage stress in our lives, how we focus, and the quality of sleep we experience.

Up to the age of approximately seven years old your brain was predominantly in the alpha and theta state of mind, which is basically a receptive hypnotic meditation mode to gather and absorb information. That is why it is not uncommon for a 5- or 6-year-old to have learned to speak four languages. These are the years that your mind develops and establishes a large array of negative neural pathways and paradigms, you learn all the negative habits your parents learned and passed to you and the bad habits, thoughts, and beliefs your culture and environment imprinted on you while in those early years. Your subconscious mind was more in everyday use absorbing and storing every experience. Once established, these bad neural pathways are then reinforced through the rest of your life. Ninety-five per cent of who you are by the time you're in your 30s is a set of unconscious thought imprints, neural pathways and paradigms imprinted within your subconscious mind. These things are all happening behind the scenes of your actual awareness. You're living your life day to day thinking this is you when you are, in fact, yes, spinning within the Matrix, living a program based on other people's principles and thoughts. After you turn seven years old, when the brain starts switching to a more beta state, the conscious/analytical mind then takes the reins and your subconscious/emotional mind though immensely more powerful, takes a very diminished role for the hours that you are awake and living.

The funny thing about the conscious, thinking, waking, reasoning mind is that it too often it gets in the way and obstructs the all-powerful subconscious mind from doing its thing. This is why meditation and mind power techniques are so key as a means to bitch slap your conscious mind, tell it to chill out, calm the fuck down and get in alignment so the subconscious mind can do its thing. Few people really understand how to reprogram the multitude of negative neural pathways already established within your mind. You need to crush the self-limiting self-sabotaging paradigms and harness the true God-given, awesome power that lies within your subconscious mind.

How is it that this great power within us is repressed and not acknowledged for its true potential and capacity?

These are just my thoughts on the matter but I believe that as we evolve the human race, more and more of the powers of the subconscious mind will be accessed. Which is to say, people in the future will be doing things with mind power that will be routine to them but for us in our time completely mind-blowing and unbelievable.

The movie *What the Bleep Do We Know!?* expertly explains how many of the ideas I present in this book are entwined with the theories of quantum physics: that there may be much more to life, us, and reality than what we are led to believe. It is generally accepted as fact now by the scientific community that it is possible to shape and effect reality with thought vibrations generated by the human mind. Some fascinating evidence of this can be seen in Dr. Masaru Emoto's work with water crystals. After being blessed with positive and loving affirmations they go from the look of molecules in disarray to beautiful symmetric shapes. Just think – if that can be done with water crystals, how can such positive affirmations and applied meditation effect and shape your life to manifest good things for you?

Let's Take a look at Quantum Physics and the ability to affect and manipulate the Quantum field with the power of our thoughts.

WHAT IS QUANTUM PHYSICS?

It is the study of the branch of physics that applies to quantum theory. Quantum theory is the theory modern physics uses to explain the makeup and behaviour of both energy and matter. This study of the nature of matter and energy is also referred to as quantum mechanics and quantum physics.

Quantum physics allows for particles to be in two states at the same time. It is a highly specialized form of science that delves much deeper than Newtonian physics. It asks the bigger questions: what is the nature of reality? How did everything come to exist and from where did everything come to exist and what exactly exists within the existing at a subatomic level?

> Quantum physics/mechanics determines every happening in your life and the surrounding world of your existence as well as things you can't see and are not yet aware of.

Quantum physics/mechanics determines every happening in your life and the surrounding world of your existence as well as things you can't see and are not yet aware of. The thing about quantum physics/mechanics is that although many don't understand it we are all immersed and soaking in it, and it can be used productively to our advantage.

This science boasts a number of bizarre phenomena – particles miles apart that can communicate with one another instantaneously, photons that without plausible explanation go two directions at the same time. Many modern-day technological advances in modern living can be attributed to the study of the science of quantum physics. This science gave birth to the laser and the invention of the transistor, evolving to the personal computer.

This science involves understanding the behavioural patterns of atoms, the interaction of matter and energy/light.

Early science fiction projected that there was going to be a revolution in energy and people would be flying around in cars without wheels and using jetpacks. We are getting there believe me, but what came first was the information revolution spawned by the Internet, creating the age of information connecting the global community. This was made possible by the use of solid-state physics, semiconductors that came to be through the science of quantum mechanics.

Unlike traditional physics that viewed the world, us, life, and everything in it as solid and physical, quantum physics explains that the roads we drive, or the fork you hold in your hand, the remote control you change channels with, are all far from solid matter. The theory is that everything is alive "energy" shifting and moving and that there is far far more to everyday reality than what we perceive.

Imagine us as a tribe hanging out on a flat plain world, and we understand everything in terms of the flat plain world experience and living. Now imagine there is a huge colossal sphere sitting on top of the flat plain world and at the point where the sphere contacts the flat plain world, the flat plain world people can interact, absorb, and experience its attributes. However, what the flat plain world people don't know is that the contact point area where they integrate with the sphere and are partially conscious of its presence and some of its attributes only represents an infinitesimally small portion of what is the entire sphere, and what the flat plain world people also don't know is that from this connection point where the sphere sits on top of the flat plain world they are immersed and integrated with all the secrets, wonder, magical power, and immensity of the entire sphere sitting on top of the flat plain world.

> The infinite intelligence resides within your subconscious mind.

The flat plain world people have evolved to a place where they can only understand so much of the sphere and as they continue to evolve their capacity to study and understand its nature, the wise all-knowing sphere reveals more of its secrets to them.

The infinite intelligence resides within your subconscious mind. The infinite intelligence also resides within your reality consciousness, which includes the universe of infinite possibilities present, past, and future, that may or may not happen. It resides where space and time are bent to a different form of reality than the way we traditionally perceive them.

To be clear, the infinite intelligence resides within every atomic and subatomic particle within the universe seen or unseen. When those waveforms of energy blink in and out of existence and go who knows exactly where the infinite intelligence is riding shotgun.

Where the universe of infinite possibilities boldly exits, you can bet that the infinite intelligence is there during their journey in and out of existence as we know it to the other side lying in wait to see which version of your personally channeled interpretation of conscious reality will win the day and manifest.

Just because our minds interpret and see, internalize everything we see, touch, taste, and smell as being a certain way, does not mean that they are as we see them. Yes folks, what I'm saying is it is just like the Transformers, life is so so much more than meets the eye.

To give you an idea and fuck with your head a bit, think about infinity. Imagine going out past the planets, going past Pluto and zooming right out of our spiral Milky Way galaxy hundreds of thousands of light years in length and then let's imagine zooming past 20 billion light years more worth of galaxies (the estimated age of the universe). Ask yourself at that point what exists? More never-ending galaxies? Eternal blackness or whiteness waiting for expanding universes to fill them up?

Can there be a wall? A stopping point where it all ends? Logical thinking makes us think that it can't possibly end. It has to keep on going forever and ever for all eternity, but how the fuck in any way is that hypothesis logical and here is where we screw with your mind in that if infinity is possible, then anything and I mean anything imagined present, past, or future in equal and opposite worlds is possible. Beginning at the atomic and subatomic levels quantum science helps determine how everything in the universe came to exist both seen and unseen.

The theory is that everything is and originated from pure energy. Top scientists of quantum theory suggest the purest form of energy is what they call waveforms. These finite little buggers aren't limited to any logical construct of shape or form. They are observed to flash in and out of existence as being there one moment and then they are gone and where the hell they go, a parallel universe perhaps, is anybody's guess. They will behave one way and then when they are aware the scientist is watching them they will perform a different way just to screw with the scientist's heads as not to be predictable. They are realized within a plain of the existence of infinite probabilities and possibilities of potential happenings and events that may or may not ever happen, which brings us back to the mind screw theory "if infinity is possible then absolutely anything imagined is possible". All possibilities, all probability future, past, or present, exists as a waveform.

Where they come from and how they exist is still somewhat of a mystery but we do know they exist. Everything at its core consists of pure energy both the physical and metaphysical. We truly are all one and come from the same source, as everything is intricately interconnected with everything else which is a continually beautiful sexy, vibrating mass of pure energy.

"Letting the days go by, let the water hold me down,
And you may tell yourself
This is not my beautiful house!
And you may tell yourself
This is not my beautiful wife!"
—Talking Heads

What's it isn't and what isn't is ... hmm
"What can you really know?
What can you really trust?
What are your doubts?
What are your certainties?
What do you call true?
When you look at the sky, what do you see?
Shadows, reflections
Distant echoes.
You see the moon as if it were there a second ago"
You see the sun as it was shining eight minutes ago
What do you really see?
Can you trust your eyes?
—Simon Silver, Robert De Niro character movie Red Lights 2012

The Newtonian physics model taught us a common sense belief that the physical world we live in is both solid and stable. Then came the quantum era to turn that thinking on its head. Through the study of quantum physics, we find that tiny particles of the matter referred to as atoms and molecules could vanish and transform to whirling clouds of energy. The science suggests that, in fact, nothing in existence is fixed or certain. This thinking that the physical world is not a given has been validated and scientifically proven.

The theory is that everything exists as a wave of invisible energy extending in all directions until it is observed by an observer. In that moment and only then is when particles and molecules materialize to assume the form they present to the viewer.

Yes, I'm saying what's going on behind your back out of your vision "for you yourself" is not actually happening till you turn around and look at it. Call me crazy but I didn't invent this theory. I'm just the messenger.

How can this be, you may ask? The consistent continuity of reality doesn't require quanta "subatomic energy waveform particles" to have any specific sequence in time. A quantum is not subject to any notion of space or time and can occupy all of its possible quantum states simultaneously. The physical world is not experienced/seen the same for everyone. Our reality and physical world as we experience it only mirrors our human nervous system.

Life is a bit fucked up, potentially volatile, and unpredictable. It doesn't play along to common sense and reason. There is no predictable, organized mathematical expression to what we consciously witness as our daily reality.

To reasonable thinking people, I can see how expressing their reality on a safe paradigm based, predictable, possibly mundane, boring, stale repetitive daily basis, that is to say, living their lives with common sense and reason, makes perfect sense. In reality, we should be guided by the force as in *Star Wars* and feel our way through life using our intuition. This thinking for some might be a bit too far out there and bordering on what they interpret as the cuckoo side of reality. And though to many it might be way out there, science discoveries of the quantum era point to the fact our conscious reality is indeed way out there and now that the cat is out of the bag there is no going back. I'm not saying there isn't a time and place for good old common sense and reason. I'm saying as you're headed down the ski hill of life, yes, negotiate the twists and turns with a game plan for success but some turns will unpredictably come out of nowhere. It is at these times that an unshakable belief that you are one with the ski hill and the ski hill is one with you, can play to your advantage. Trust in the knowledge that everything in existence is pure energy. We are intrinsically connected to everything as it is to us. Everything in existence came from the same source. We can put trust in this truth that our human consciousness creates our physical world and can manipulate the physical world the way we envision it to be, jump, knowing the safety net is there and the force will have your back as well as guide your way through the universe of probability and dual reality.

The idea of human consciousness creating our physical reality or at least to say how each one of us perceives our reality is not everyone's cup of tea. Many people, including some very smart and influential people that I hold in high regard such as the late Jim Rohn, would speak and teach the life-changing advantage gained in goal setting and the disciplines required to live an inspired life and really go after what is your passion. But they stop short of declaring that people can bend, shape, and modify their physical reality with the power of their thoughts.

Author Napoleon Hill absolutely believed in these principal truths decades before modern science showed them to at least be very plausible if not valid. Back in the day, especially, our modern day pioneer and law of attraction mentor and hero was thought of, portrayed, and ridiculed as quite the whack job, nutbar, and a little bit cuckoo. Within today's scientific community there exist, understandably, conflicting beliefs and perspectives of different scientific theories concerning quantum mechanics/physics understanding that it is still a relatively new science. What is certain is that to understand an infinite reality, which is exactly what reality is, we would need an infinite human nervous system, which of course we do not possess.

Our lives play out trucking through the quantum field of reality. The more self-aware and enlightened you are, the more you are a player rather than an also-ran. The also-rans enjoyed the ride yes, but perhaps never really got the full jist of just what the hell was going on. Maybe near the end of the ride or perhaps purposefully and blissfully, they remained oblivious of the whole spiel of the deal of the mysterious and magical roller coaster ride of human theatre that in its entirety reflects what is ,was, and will be their lives' experience. The question you want to ask yourself is the question posed by the brilliant Roger Waters in the song *Wish You Were Here*, and that is do you want "a lead role in a cage", the cage being a self-imposed prison of the Matrix replaying a program on autopilot, or do you want "a walk on part in the war", as in get in there and mix it up, break free and get connected to the source energy, become truly alive.

I love this gem from Author Wayne Dyer: "We are not human beings having a spiritual experience, we are spiritual beings having a human experience."

Let's talk about the experience of *qualia*.

The term qualia from a Latin word meaning for "what sort" or "what kind" is a philosophical term used to refer to subjective conscious experiences. This terminology of neuroscience refers to our experience of the senses: the colours we see, the sounds we hear, the textures we feel, all that we experience in this way can be referred to as qualia.

Every human experience, from watching a bright red sunset, to tasting and enjoying some cognac and a good cigar is all qualia. The existence of certain attributes of qualia is debated – amounts – by various theoreticians and philosophers. For the purpose of this book, I'm saying that all qualia are created in your consciousness. Your brain is a quantum device that processes the experience of qualia.

Quantum physics says every particle/ molecule in existence is flashing in and out of the void at a rapid rate – thousands of times per second. The void is referred to in many ways: The pre-created universe, the vacuum state, the field of all probabilities, the intergalactic space of mindfucking wowness (that one's mine).

More real than the physical universe that we experience and know is the plain of infinite potential and probability, where the potential reality of all events future, past, and present exist. Absolutely any thought or situation, or happening we can conceive of resides within the plain of infinite potential. For this reason, for the human mind to perceive real authentic reality, we would need as I mentioned to be equipped with an infinite nervous system. Instead, we perceive reality with what we have, which is the latest evolved edition of human consciousness.

You are the source of your own qualia. You are the caretaker of your own consciousness. You control the power to bring whatever you want/desire into your life experience. The plain of infinite probability is there waiting for you to grab the reins and command the reality that's in your best interest.

In the closing of this chapter

Believe me for real, through meditation and the practice of mind power you can become self-aware and increase the influential vibration of your immensely powerful subconscious mind to connect to the quantum field of existence and manipulate it to manifest your aspirations and desires of abundance. Your rate of vibration dictates your rate of connection and manipulation. To raise your frequency and get maximum vibration you need proper mind and body alignment: healthy, exercised, hydrated and focussed. You need to be free of modern-day inhibitors and blockers and distractors of your vibration. You must reach within and amp up/supercharge your desire, your faith, your focus of visualization with relentless persistence and undying belief the result being – you simply cannot be stopped from what it is you desire. You will become a human equivalent of a running freight train of manifestation power to change and manipulate physical reality with the power of your channeled and projected thoughts.

Chapter 11

Money May Not Buy Happiness but Having Lots of it Certainly Doesn't Suck

Yes the fact remains as the Beatles sang so many years ago "money can't buy you love", but on the flip side, "broke ass doesn't buy shit".

If through the process of going from broke ass guy/girl to rich ass guy/girl you become an enlightened self-aware and empowered individual, the prize you have attained is not the riches you've acquired but in fact the person you have developed and become to make the riches. You could, in theory, toss the riches away and after some time make it all back because you've developed the mindset and disciplines needed to attain financial independence.

You cannot get rich while feeling poor.

This is why if you took all the world's money and distributed it amongst everybody equally, eventually the money will return to the rich people and the broke ass people will return to broke ass because they are not equipped with prosperity consciousness.

You alone are responsible for your abundance. You chart your path with your feelings and beliefs towards money whether you create wealth or not. You cannot get rich while feeling poor.

If you want to make real money you're going to have to entertain the idea of being an entrepreneur, risky yes but you gotta be willing to stick your neck out to some degree to attain bigger successes in life.

The safety and comfort of a job traps you at J.O.B.:"Just over broke."

Working to make others rich is not going to get you there. Are you working for money or is money working for you?

Working hard is not the way to make big money. Having a dedicated work ethic, yes but the actual truth is that hard work is the worst way to earn money. Riches, when they come in huge quantities, are never the result of HARD work they are the result of SMART work!

> "Riches come, if they come at all, in response to definite
> demands, based upon the application of definite principles,
> and not by chance or luck."
> —Napolean Hill, *Think and Grow Rich*

Most everybody dreams of being rich and having the freedom to do anything they want to do but usually, it doesn't go much further than dreaming of winning the lottery. Making large amounts of money it is not as hard to do as most people are conditioned to think it is.

The people with lots of money are fine with the fact that most people haven't acquired the skills and disciplines to create wealth and financial independence because they believe if they did, the small per cent of people that control most of the money would have a lot less money. The reality is that you personally can't get rich enough that you're going to make anyone poor and you personally can't be poor enough to make anyone rich.

In order to attract money into your experience, you must replace your negative and limiting beliefs related to money. Identify your limiting beliefs about money, what they are, and replace them with what would benefit you. There's a prevalent idea within society that the poor get poorer and the rich get richer and the reason is not that of competition; there is no competition for resources in an infinite universe.

The reason that the poor get poorer and the rich get richer is because poor people are born into environments that have a lot of attitudes and beliefs about money, which doesn't benefit them or invites finance and by focusing on those realities and by focusing those beliefs they manifest more evidence, which proves their own lack of abundance to them. That's why the poor get poorer and sustain a "poverty consciousness". The rich get richer because they are aware of their own abundance. It's not a question they are entitled to it. They don't have thoughts that limit them relative to money so regardless of how much they lose or gain, they sustain a "prosperity consciousness".

We create and are personally responsible for everything that happens to us. No one else is responsible for your abundance, nobody else is taking it away from you, you alone are responsible with your feelings and beliefs towards money whether you manifest riches or not.

FOCUS ON GRATITUDE

You must work your way into the vibrational vicinity of feeling like you've already achieved wealth and abundance. The best way to do this is by focusing on gratitude. Feel the gratefulness and fulfilling feeling of having what you want like it's already happened. To be in the vibration of gratitude for all the things that are going well in your life right now, pure positive appreciation for things that are in your life already, that is the exact vibration of wealth and abundance. If you can focus on gratitude every day you're opening up the wellspring of abundance to have money flow into your life and let's face it, money is not really what we want. It is the things that money can help us get.

You need to visualize what you want and what it is you want to do with the money. Get as elaborate and detailed as you possibly can. Ask yourself why you want these things. The universe responds to the why and the what you want to do with the money more than it does your idea about money.

It has to be believable to you, make it as real as you can – the house, the car, the boat, the lifestyle – envision it as if you can taste, touch, sense, and feel it but make it believable. This is key. If it's not believable to you, what you're going to be feeling when you go to the visualization is 'I want that but I don't think I can really have it'. This is a detrimental visualization. Think of the thoughts that make you feel good relative to the money that is believable for you.

Self-analyze, root out, and replace your mixed and limiting beliefs about money related to the subject of money. Shift these beliefs so that your relationship and your association will attract money if you want money to flow into your life experience. Money is just a tool. It can be an incredibly valuable tool so the love of money in itself is not the root of all evil it can be your tool for freedom within society to choose to do what it is you want.

Are you ready to commit to raising your positive vibration to acquire and attract money? If you're going to attract money you must then consciously line up with the decision. You can't do something that you think will detract from your abundance and maintain wealth. If you have debt find ways to eliminate it. Debt makes you focus on the lack. You don't want to act from a space of need. You want the opportunities to flow to you and then take the action when it feels good to take it.

Most people think they don't deserve things. Get in the mind space of believing in thinking that you do deserve. In society today, we have this idea that entitlement is this horribly negative thing, yet expectation, as I've mentioned in previous chapters, is key to success. Through entitlement, we think that we're taking from someone else's joy and abundance but entitlement is something we have to shift our consciousness to believe and accept is relative to because the minute you incarnate onto this planet you are entitled to receive the manifestation of anything you can dream of. It is, in fact, your birthright. You already deserve it. You already are entitled to it. You're entitled to anything you can think or dream of. You have to shift to an attitude of deserving.

Self-love is necessary to get to the vibrational vicinity to attract wealth, feeling as if you can have money the way it was intended to come to you. Not through the avenue of intense effort, though the effort is needed but through the avenue of intense focus IE Bill Gates, Warren Buffet.

Make a budget, cut unnecessary expenses to help you lineup.

Think of money as purely being energy.

Trust in the universe and trust that it will happen for you. Don't focus on the ways; it has not yet manifested. Start visualizing and think of yourself as a money magnet.

To become a money magnet understand this: money is energy and as such it has no limits. Energy moves freely towards what is most alike. Like all energy, it harmonizes with like energy to be a money magnet. To be attracted to money you must learn to vibrate in harmony with the energy that is money and then you'll become a money magnet. Stop thinking about money as anything other than energy. Don't think of it as being security. Don't think of it as being wealth. Don't think of it as being freedom or any of the actions that are typically associated with money. Think of money as purely being energy. You must learn how to vibrate in harmony with that energy. Start by doing little things. For example, increase your belief levels that you are in fact a money magnet. Start imagining that every single day money is going to start coming into your experience, in one way or another. Don't define it and cash will start coming into your life – real spendable currency.

If you're serious about making money, there are steps that must be taken that most people simply do not do. It's common knowledge you're not going to get rich working for somebody else.

> "If you don't find a way to make money while you sleep, you will work until you die."
> —Warren Buffet

You're going to need to have the courage to take a risk and embrace the mindset of an entrepreneur. Find your niche market where there's a demand for what you do, become extremely good at what you do so that you are not easily replaced. While you're creating your plan of action to acquire riches you might want to be sure you're not unconsciously holding yourself back.

Why do the majority of people not become rich? Well, for the majority of people it simply never occurs to them to become wealthy.

The average person grows up in an environment where they've never known anybody personally that's made tons of money. They go through school and socialize with people who are not wealthy, then out of school work with people that are not wealthy, and their social circle outside of work consists of people that are not wealthy and they have no mentors or role models who are wealthy.

Think of the five people in your life that you are closest to and spend the most time with. You can add up each person's yearly income and chances are they will be relatively the same. The reality is that it's just as possible for the average person to become wealthy as much as anyone else.

We are the company we keep; if you want to be successful you need to associate and interact with successful people and absorb their tendencies and habits. Finding a mentor or mentors to observe and learn from is key to your financial success. Check out all the great successful people throughout history and you will see that with their aid in becoming great they all had great mentors.

Get out there and seek mentorship from people who have created wealth. Make friendships and spend as much time socializing and learning from them as possible.

You must be intentional and make the decision that you want to become wealthy. You must set goals and take dedicated action. If you continue to do what you've always done, you'll continue to get what you've always got. Spinning wheels and procrastinating will never get it done. You've got to get inside your state of being and develop new habits and initiate behavioural changes.

As the days roll by, you wake up each day, brush your teeth, you go to work, you get home, crack a beer, have something to eat and turn on the boob tube. Those thoughts of taking action towards starting that business and your plans for creating wealth gets lost in the maze of procrastination. There's no shortage of reasons why now is not the right time to take action and put it off, and your broke ass friends will be only too glad to help encourage you to stay broke ass and tell you exactly why none of your ideas or aspirations will work. Not everyone's going to negatively criticize and shoot down your dreams and plans for financial independence, but you would be amazed how many negative nellies come down the pike compared to the few that will offer words of encouragement.

For this reason, you need to work your plan and plan your work and for the most part keep it to yourself as opposed to announcing and bragging about all the great things you're going to do because for the most part, the feedback you solicit will be negative, not to mention that someone might steal your plan.

Enemy number one for personal change towards the dedicated daily practice of meditation in mind power, or an action plan for acquiring financial independence is procrastination.

Suppose a friend called you up and said they have a couple extra tickets for you and your partner to join them on an all-expense paid vacation to a tropical paradise. All you have to do is meet them at the airport in four days' time. You tell your partner about the great news and at that moment you look at each other and say, "Holy crap, if we're going to make that happen we have to get this that and a host of other things done" within the four-day period of time. You put your heads together and make it happen and meet your friend at the airport very impressed with yourselves and even a little shocked with how you were able to become so highly motivated to accomplish all those tasks within that short period of time.

The fact is, day after day, so much more can be accomplished than what gets done because of our familiar nemesis procrastination. Practice pretending that at the end of each week you're going on that vacation and that your list of things to get done gets done aggressively and efficiently with discipline.

For many people, they get some inspiration and a mindset they can become wealthy and want to become wealthy and take that first step to make a decision to change. Procrastination can come along and blast all their plans into the indefinite future and nothing will ever happen.

A great exercise for prosperity consciousness is to take ten per cent of every paycheque, money coming in and put it aside for savings. Sounds simple enough but you would be surprised how this one practice helps lock you into prosperity consciousness.

When I was a little kid, the money I got from mowing lawns in the neighbourhood I would spend immediately on junk food and whatever. Whereas in contrast, my brother would save the money he earned and then acquire really cool stuff like a dirt bike and a fancy leather jacket. So many people in adult life cannot delay their need for gratification. Most people can't resist the temptation to spend every single dime they make or worse go for the 'get it now with no money down start paying the higher interest payments later' deals, borrowing and buying on credit. If you can't discipline yourself from spending everything you make and even worse racking up credit cards and high-interest debt, you simply cannot become wealthy.

The fact is, if you cannot save money and practice budgeting as a lifelong habit, financial independence is not in the cards for you. Successfully making money, of course, takes advantage of the principles of the law of attraction and manipulating the quantum field to your advantage through applied mind power.

A Prosperity Consciousness must be developed if you're going to be successful building your fortune. The basis of prosperity consciousness is that like energy attracts like energy. Once again we meet at the crossroads where we attract into our life what we are focused on, good or bad. And for many, they are not focused on the right things because bad habits and self-imposed barriers that have been cultivated into their subconscious mind throughout their lifetime. As mentioned previously, so many are spinning around in the Matrix on mental auto-pilot. This negative process is in action continuously as we do it mostly unconsciously and the joke is on us because we are not self-aware as to what is going on.

So many people have the wrong attitude about money, that it corrupts and people that have lots, must have screwed others along the way to getting it. They develop a "poverty consciousness" that hooks into their psychology.

The qualities and mindset needed to help you achieve your goals are the same qualities needed for great leadership. If you chose the path of entrepreneur to make your fortune, you're going to need great leadership skills and surround yourself with talented people. Great leadership skills inspire and persist and will be key to your personal growth and success. You might think the top leaders and CEOs of big organizations and corporations are highly animated, Mensa smart, highly energetic and charismatic people. But that is actually not often the case. They are, however, focused and highly functional individuals.

Maybe you're not a team leader or business owner yet but these traits and mindsets of effective leaders are good learning for anyone. Here is a quick synopsis of some major leadership qualities

CONFIDENCE

There will always be times when things don't run smoothly. Don't ever let panic set in. Be calm and rock solid, assure everyone that setbacks will naturally come and go and maintain that most important is to keep a focus on the larger goal.

COMMUNICATION

Knowing what it is what you want to be accomplished but you must also be accomplished at being able to communicate this to others.

DELEGATE

The vision of how you see your company/brand is essential to creating a well-organized and efficient business. You must be able to have trust in your team and assemble quality people. By having quality people involved with assistance in the day to day tasks you can stay on top of your business machine rather than bogged down within the day to day tasks that other quality people can help you with. As your business grows, delegating tasks to the right people is a most important skill. If you let tasks pile up and stretch yourself thin, your business will suffer in quality and production.

HONESTY

Your word is your bond, and you set the standard so "lead by example". When you're leading a team, the ethics bar gets raised higher. If you're honest and accountable then your team will follow suit. Your business, as well as employees, are a direct reflection of the standard you set.

COMMITMENT

There's nothing more inspiring than to see the boss in the trenches working hard amongst everyone else. With this effective move you not only establish some street cred but you also inject good energy throughout your people. There is no better way to motivate them to jump out in front of the troops and spearhead the charge.

APPROACH

To get the best from the team you need to be able to access how to react to and cultivate the members on a person to person basis. Everyone is different and will require personalized strategies to be effective.

POSITIVE ATTITUDE

A state of mind and emotions that drag and run down positive energy are very noticeable within a team environment, resulting in low-level Debbie Downer energy. Seek to maintain a positive attitude and energy level.

CREATIVITY

The developed skills of creativity and imagination are tools no good leader can be without.

Sometimes you'll have to make a decision and both your options are bad ones. You have to identify if that is indeed the case and choose the least bad of the two or source your creative energy to think outside the box to find the third and better alternative, giving the issues some time for thought and then try to come to a decisive decision.

INTUITION

When the future is uncertain and you're leading a team in and through unchartered waters,

there will be a higher risk and heavier pressure. This is the time smart and properly applied natural intuition can make or break the situation.

INSPIRE

Inspiring your people to have a sense of the success to come especially during the lean times of a start-up is vital. Put some incentives such as a piece of owner equity or a bonus system in place. Give recognition and appreciation for individual efforts and hard work.

> If you can figure out how to stay broke, you can figure out how to get rich.

People that become millionaires do not make excuses. They look for opportunities, and they seize them. They seize the moment with purpose, and they never quit. If you want to be prosperous then you must train your mind to focus on prosperity. And your focus will be broken up and disrupted by the negative paradigms until you aggressively deal with them.

In order to attract money into your experience, you must replace your negative and limiting beliefs about money with a new money positive perspective that benefits you.

First, identify what does success and prosperity mean to you. Think in terms that all obstacles are removed, and your success is guaranteed like a genie granting your wish. Then close your eyes and create an image in your mind that you're living your dream.

This is the fun part! Practice it daily: write the things you plan to acquire and the lifestyle you plan to live in your journal and empower those aspirations with the magic and power of the written word. Also make a large vision board and cut out and paste the things you wish to acquire: sailboat, home in the Mediterranean, private helicopter, super-car, etc. Then visualize driving the supercar at high speed and hearing the sonic growl of its 800 horsepower engine. Visualize being out on your sailboat with friends on a gorgeous sunny day and the smell of the sea air.

Even better, go to the local Ferrari or Maserati dealer and take one for a spin. Go to an open house for what represents your dream home and walk around visualizing it being yours. Do you want tons of money in the bank? How much money is your target? What is the lifestyle you envision and how much money flow will be required to sustain such a lifestyle? Do you want to own certain kinds of properties or build a large company? The ultimate goal is to feel fulfilled and happy, with peace of mind and love and contentment in your heart.

Making lots of money does not suck that is for sure but it far from guarantees happiness and inner peace. Acquiring lots of money can bring many issues and challenges. Many people become overwhelmed. That's why so many lottery winners return to broke and are less happy than before they won. You gotta worry about how to keep it, who are the people you can trust, etc. That said, having lots of money gives you freedom to do the things you're passionate about and most importantly you can become a "super giver" when you've acquired lots and lots to give back to those that can be helped and are in need. The mindset of being a giver is essential to prosperity consciousness because when you give without any strings or agenda of getting something back the universe will open up and shower you with prosperity. The key is you must not think of the getting when you are giving. Know in your mind with a confidence that givers will always be rewarded and give selflessly.

What you don't do is go out do your giving then say to the universe, ok I did my giving so gimme gimme my getting! The universe/infinite intelligence will see right through this and deposit a lump of black coal in your Christmas stocking as opposed to riches.

The bad habits and negative paradigms must be discovered within your subconscious, identified, isolated, and dealt with and then new actions and beliefs that are in alignment with prosperity consciousness must be introduced. The most effective tools to achieve this are through meditation, positive affirmations, and exercises that will nourish your mind and spirit. Daily practice will transform you into alignment with the actions and habits that will draw prosperity into your life.

Many people are hooked to a poverty consciousness slave to negative neutral pathways riddled throughout their subconscious mind. Be aware that these little bastards exist and are actively engaged in blocking your potential success. These attitudes and thought forms don't represent you they represent a belief system of other people, your parents and Western culture in general. Last but not least a super tip for supercharging the process of acquiring wealth and financial independence. Once you have developed a healthy expectation that you will achieve your goal and mapped out a solid plan of action, you must marry this expectation with the feeling of gratitude in the mindset and feeling that you have already achieved your goal. Gratitude every day for all the things in your life that you have to be grateful for but also develop the feeling of gratitude for the desired outcome that is yet to be achieved with the visualization and mindset that it has already been achieved and it's already yours. Do this to the best of your ability on a daily basis and reap big-time results.

IN CLOSING

My friends, you are truly powerful! I urge you to embrace the power within. My best advice is from *Star Wars*: "You are one with the force, and the force is one with you."

It's true that many and most people are not aware of the powers of meditation, the powers of the subconscious mind and that most people live their lives hypnotized, running a program on Matrix autopilot.

Modern society spins people through the carousel of paradigms and schema scripts like puppet people being forced to fit and conform to social ideals.

We lose focus of who we really are and our authentic self is suppressed. We become pretenders to fit in, trapped in this invisible illusion Matrix. We find ourselves living in the age of unlightenment instead of enlightenment

But I do believe the tide is slowly turning as the upcoming millennial generation is becoming more aware and asking questions and challenging antiquated belief systems. It's a theory, but I believe as many others do that there is a strong intellectual division going on right now in the world. Every single paradigm right now in this particular time in history is collapsing the very same way the polar ice caps are from global warming.

whether it's the political, economic, religious, environmental, medical, or the educational model. All the systems are breaking down because basically, for lack of me providing a better expression, it hasn't worked for shit up until this point. Some people, mostly the aging generations, will cling to the familiar old school ways, to what they think works. Hanging on to those antiquated belief systems, simply put, it's the dumbass way and it's wrong.

If we can embrace a new model and a new way of doing things we can begin to create a better way, to promote global unity and harmony, to bring out the best in people. When we begin to be the change and we begin to modify our behaviors towards self awareness and unified global awareness. We begin to upscale our genetics resonating higher more powerful brain function through neural plasticity. We evolve towards a new collective global consciousness and awareness in the realization that we are all connected brother and sisters and come from the same universal source energy. Hopefully our global community will come together powered by a collective consciousness of love, caring, understanding, and nurturing for one another and the earth we inhabit and all the earth animals and creatures that share this miraculous existence with us.

I encourage you to jump in, take a stand, to have an opinion, and be counted. We sit at a historical crossroad, the ice caps are melting and species are being wiped out at an unprecedented and alarming rate. The evidence is clear. The Earth itself might go on just fine but we as a civilization are on the fast track to destruction and extinction through industrialized greed and a lack of caring and management of this earth that is our home If we are going to turn the tide, the time for aggressive action to that end is now. This is the time in geological history when humans are the major force shaping the physical-chemical and biological properties of the planet. We are the force that is determining where the planet itself is going.

It is believed by some scientists and people in the know that the shitstorm is coming within the next 30 to 40 years to where our global quality of life will be comparable to the inhabitants of Easter Island after every resource had been used up and they were reduced to living in caves and cannibalism. What can you do you might ask? Think globally and act locally, develop good loving energy within yourself and your own consciousness then actively spread it through your community, be kind to others and express love be it an act of kindness or simply a smile. Be conscious of your own personal ecological impact to the environment: recycle, buy an electric car, drive less, become a vegetarian or practice eating less meat. Do volunteer work within your community. Go online right now and become a supporting member of the Global Citizen movement at www.globalcitizen.org and become an active member. Or support Playing For Change at www.playingfor-change.com.

Support PETA and charities you feel worthy. Most of all use your vote for political parties and candidates that are truly committed to ecological sustainability not controlled or ruled by big industry and big money interests. My personal preference is the Green Party. I agree with their charter and their values.

I invite you to check out the following principles I've included here and decide for yourself if they are in line with your beliefs as they are mine.

Green Party Charter

Recognizing the limited scope for the material expansion of society within the biosphere, and the need to maintain biodiversity through the use of renewable resources.

Participatory Democracy

Striving for a democracy in which all citizens have the right to express their views, and are able to directly participate in decisions which affect their lives.

Respect for Diversity

We honor and value equally the Earth's biological and ecological diversity together with the context of individual responsibility toward all beings.

Ecological Wisdom

This world is finite, therefore unlimited material growth is impossible. Ecological sustainability is paramount. We acknowledge that human beings are part of the natural world and we respect the specific value of all forms of life, including non-human species. Recognizing the scope for the material expansion of society within the biosphere, and the need to maintain biodiversity through the use of renewable resources.

Social Responsibility

Unlimited material growth is impossible. Therefore the key to social responsibility is the just distribution of social and natural resources, both locally and globally. Asserting that the key to social responsibility is the equitable distribution of resources to ensure that all have full opportunities for personal and social development.

Appropriate Decision-making

For the implementation of ecological wisdom and social responsibility, decisions will be made directly at the appropriate level by those affected.

Non-Violence

Non-violent conflict resolution is the process by which ecological wisdom, social responsibility and appropriate decision making will be implemented. This principle applies at all levels. Declaring a commitment to non-violence and strive for a culture of peace and cooperation between states.

No matter which political party you agree with, have your vote be counted and be a part of the process.

I would like to thank you, dear reader, for purchasing my book. I hope the content was both entertaining and of help to you. I urge you, don't wake up each day and think 'here I go again through the mundane familiar paces unappreciated by all and slave to my existence' get real about it and take a good look around. The beauty and magnificence is right in front of you if you care to remove the blinders and be witness to the fact your every living breathing moment is an incredible mind-fucking miracle. Grab a hold, don't waste the gift, jump in getting excited and may the force be with you.

I wish you all the best fortune along your journey whether it be to improve relationships, lose some stress, rid some bad habits, make some more money, enjoy life more, or complete spiritual transcendental enlightenment. To you, my universal brother or sister, I wish peace, love, tranquility, and a friendly 'get out there and make it happen', slap on the ass.

> "I know you're out there. I can feel you now. I know that you're afraid ... you're afraid of us. You're afraid of change. I don't know the future. I didn't come here to tell you how this is going to end. I came here to tell you how it's going to begin. I'm going to hang up this phone, and then I'm going to show these people what you don't want them to see. I'm going to show them a world without you. A world without rules and controls. Without borders or boundaries. A world where anything is possible. Where we go from there is a choice I leave to you."
> —Neo, *The Matrix*

CPSIA information can be obtained
at www.ICGtesting.com
Printed in the USA
LVHW011940090519
617327LV00001B/26

9 781525 510182